The Extant Poetical Works of William Lauder,

Playwright, Poet, and Minister of the Word of God.

1

I. Ane Compendious and Brebe Tractate concernyng the Office and Dewtie of Kyngis, Spirituall Pastoris, and Temporall Jugis. A.D. 1556.

EDITED BY

FITZEDWARD HALL, M.A., Hon. D.C.L. Oxon.

2

II. Ane Godlie Tractate or Mirrour (*showing who are grafted into Christ, and who not; exposing the Devilish Doctrine of the Papists; and denouncing the Swinish & Hellish Greediness of the False Protestants*)

III. The Lamentatioun of the Pure, twiching the Miserabill Estait of this present World, 1 Febr. 1568.

3

IV. Ane Prettie Mirrour or Conference bettwix the faithfull Protestant and the Dissemblit False Hypocreit.

V. Ane trew & breue Sentencius Descriptioun of the Nature of Scotland twiching the Interteinment of Virtewus Men that laketh Riches.

VI. Ane Gude Exempill be the Butterflie, instructing Men to hait all Harlottrie.

EDITED BY

F. J. FURNIVALL, M.A., Trin. Hall, Camb.

LONDON:
PUBLISHED FOR THE EARLY ENGLISH TEXT SOCIETY,
BY N. TRÜBNER & CO., 60, PATERNOSTER ROW.

MDCCCLXX.

Ane Compendious

And breve Tractate, Concernyng ye Office and dewtie of Kyngis, Spirituall Pastoris, and temporall Iugis Laitlie Compylit be William Lauder. For the faithfull Instructioun of Kyngis, and Prencis.

Diligite Iusticiam qui iudicatis terram.

The Minor Poems

of

William Lauder.

DUBLIN:	WILLIAM McGEE, 18, NASSAU STREET.
EDINBURGH:	T. G. STEVENSON, 22, SOUTH FREDERICK STREET.
GLASGOW:	OGLE & CO., 1, ROYAL EXCHANGE SQUARE.
BERLIN:	ASHER & CO., UNTER DEN LINDEN, 11.
BOSTON, U.S.:	DUTTON & CO.
NEW YORK:	C. SCRIBNER & CO.; LEYPOLDT & HOLT.
PHILADELPHIA:	J. B. LIPPINCOTT & CO.

The Minor Poems

of

William Lauder,

Playwright, Poet, and Minister of the Word of God,

(*mainly on the State of Scotland in and about* 1568 A.D.,
that year of Famine and Plague).

1

I. Ane Goodlie Tractate or Mirrour (*showing who are grafted into Christ, and who not; exposing the Devilish Doctrine of the Papists; and denouncing the Swinish & Hellish Greediness of the False Protestants*)

II. The Lamentatioun of the Pure, twiching the Miserabill Estait of this present World, 1 Febr. 1568.

2

III. Ane Prettie Mirrour or Conference betwix the faithfull Protestant and the Dissemblit False Hypocreit.

IV. Ane trew & breue Sentencius Descriptioun of the Nature of Scotland twiching the Interteinment of Virtewous Men that laketh Riches.

V. Ane Gude Exempill be the Butterflie, instructing Men to hait all Harlottrie.

EDITED FROM THE UNIQUE ORIGINALS BELONGING TO
S. CHRISTIE-MILLER, ESQ., OF BRITWELL,

BY

F. J. FURNIVALL, M.A., TRIN. HALL, CAMB.,

EDITOR OF 'BALLADS AND POEMS ON THE CONDITION OF ENGLAND IN HENRY VIII'S AND
EDWARD VI'S REIGNS (INCLUDING THE STATE OF THE CLERGY, MONKS, AND FRIARS), &C. &C.'

LONDON:
PUBLISHED FOR THE EARLY ENGLISH TEXT SOCIETY,
BY N. TRÜBNER & CO., 60, PATERNOSTER ROW.

MDCCCLXX.

OXFORD
UNIVERSITY PRESS

Great Clarendon Street, Oxford OX2 6DP
United Kingdom

Oxford University Press is a department of the University of Oxford.
It furthers the University's objective of excellence in research, scholarship,
and education by publishing worldwide. Oxford is a registered trade mark of
Oxford University Press in the UK and in certain other countries

© The Early English Text Society 1870

The moral rights of the authors have been asserted

Database right Oxford University Press (maker)

First Edition published in 1870

All rights reserved. No part of this publication may be reproduced,
stored in a retrieval system, or transmitted, in any form or by any means,
without the prior permission in writing of Oxford University Press,
or as expressly permitted by law, or under terms agreed with the appropriate
reprographics rights organization. Enquiries concerning reproduction
outside the scope of the above should be sent to the Rights Department,
Oxford University Press, at the address above

You must not circulate this book in any other form
and you must impose this same condition on any acquirer

Published in the United States of America by Oxford University Press
198 Madison Avenue, New York, NY 10016, United States of America

British Library Cataloguing in Publication Data
Data available

Library of Congress Cataloging in Publication Data
Data available

Original Series, 41

ISBN 978-0-85-991723-0

PREFACE.

LET us give the first place to this fresh information concerning Lauder, by the writer to whom the Preface to our first poem by that author owes all its worth.

Additional Note, by Mr Laing.[1]

In the notices of WILLIAM LAUDER prefixed to the edition of his *Compendious Tractate* by the Early English Text Society in 1864, I happened to overlook the earliest mention of the name of this old Scottish Poet which occurs in the Treasurer's Accounts.

After the death of King James Vth in December, 1542, leaving an only daughter, Mary Queen of Scots, an infant of a few days old; James, Second Earl of Arran (created by the King of France Duke of Chatellerault, in 1548) was chosen Regent or Governor of Scotland; he being declared as next in succession to the Crown, had the young Queen died without issue.

It is easy, therefore, to suppose that the nuptials of his eldest daughter, Lady Barbara Hamilton, in 1549, would be celebrated with more than ordinary splendour. Accordingly we find in these Accounts several payments connected with this marriage in February, 1548-9. One was[2],

Item, to Williame Lauder, for making of his Play, and expensis maid thereupon xj *li* v. *s* (£11 5 *s.*)

But no indication is given of the character of the Play. It was, most likely, a kind of pageant.

---

[1] The half-page below is printed also on p. xi of the Second and revised Edition of the *Office*, 1869.   [2] See p. vii.

In connection with this happy event, the following extracts from the Treasurer's Accounts may be of interest to some readers, while they serve to correct an error which is repeated in the various Peerages of Scotland, and Genealogies of the Hamilton Family.

COMPOT. THESAUR. 1546—1550. (General Register House.)

Expensis debursit be my Lord Gouernouris preceptis and speciall command.

1548 Item, ix. Augussti, to my Lord Gouernouris eldest douchter, Lady Barbara, at hir passing to the court to the Quennis grace, to be hir ane goun. vij. elnis fyne blak welwote, price of the eln, iij.*li*. iiij *s*.   *Summa,* xxv *li* iiij *s*

— November. We find entered, be the Governouris command, several furnishings for claithis to his Graces servitour Jacobus Narratius Francheman quha wes ordainit to await upoun his Graces eldest douchter and my Lord Gordoun hir spouse to lerne and instruct thame.

— The Quenis Grace [Mary Queen of Scots] being suspect of the Pest, the Treasurer paid for the expensis of his Graces douchter Lady Barbara, eight dayis in Alexander Guthries chalmer in the Castle-hill, being with hir in cumpany with three other gentlewomen with thair servantis   ij *li* xix *s* iiij *d*

— December. Ane rob ryall of purpure welwote [velvet] to Lady Barbara, aganis hir mariage; and various other articles of dress.

1548-9 January. Item to the Goldsmythis to be maid in ringes targettis and otherris toyes to be given at the mariage of Lady Barbara   J^{c}xix *li* v *s*

— Item to the Goldsmythis for the warkmanship of thir crownis quhilk wes maid in 12 targettis 10 taiblattis and hartis 5 pair of braislaittis ane chene and 30 ringis   xxxvij *li* xij *s* viij *d*

Item, a gown of quhite dalmes begaryed with quhyte welwote to Elizabeth Hammiltoun douchter to vmquhil James Hammiltoun of Stanehous aganis the day of Lady Barbaras mariage, &c.

— Various payments for furnishings for clothes to the Lady Barbara, amang which is a fine tannye welwote gown with syde tailis.

— Also for clothes to my Lord Gordoun; along with furnishings given to my Lady Huntley to be disponit in lyfrayes at the mariage.

1548-9	Item gevin to the Lady Barbara to offer, the day of hir mariage	xxij *s* vj *d*
—	Item to the Quenis Grace Tailȝeour for making of Lady Barbaras claithis	xj *li* xviij *s* ix *d*
—	Item to his servant in drinksilver	xiiij *s*
—	February. Item to foure Duchemen, quha with thair trumbis playit before Lady Barbara, at hir incuming fra the kirk	xj *li* v *s*.
	Item, to Monsr. Dersyeis four trumpettis in ix crownes of the Sone	x *li* ij *s* vj *d*.
	Item, to the Quennis Violarris	xj *li* v *s*
	Item, to ane Fydlar, quha playit at the mariage	x *s*.
	Item, be my lorde Gouvernoures speciall commande, gevyn in name of touchar,[1] with his Graces eldest douchter, mareit upoun the Lorde Gordoun, the sowme of v^m (5000) markis; quhairof rebaitit to the Erle of Huntlie, restand be his L. of the pensioun of Aberdene 3000 markis, sua only 2000 markis payit	ij^m iij^c xxxiij [*li*] vj *s* viij *d*
—	Item, be my Lordis precept to Helene Ross, to stanche hir bairdre and ewill toung.[2]	
	Item, be his Graces commande to his Graces Scrybe, Neill Laing, to by him claithis	xxij *li*
	Item, to Williame Lauder, for making of his play and expensis maid thairupon	xi *li* v *s*.
—	*March.* Item, to Lady Barbara at her departing to the Northland to put in her purs, xi crownis of the sone.	xlv *li*
1549	April. Item, be my Lorde Gouernores speciall commande to James Dalzell, quhilk he debursit vpoun the porter luge of his Graces place in Edinburgh, preparing of the keching and other necessaris of the said place, aganis the mariage of Lady Barbara	xx *li* x*s* vj *d*
1551-2	Item, xiij^s. Januarij be my Lord Gouernoures speciale command deliuerit to my Lord Gordoun to support his expensis	I^c *li*.

The Duke of Chatellerault continued at the head of affairs until he was constrained to resign the Regency, and on the 12th of April, 1554, the Queen Dowager, Mary of Guise, was proclaimed Regent of Scotland. From that time, any payments connected with his own person or family cease to appear in the Treasurer's Accounts.

From the preceding extracts there cannot be the least doubt

---

[1] For *tocher*, or marriage portion.
[2] To stop her abusive and evil speech.

that Lady Barbara's husband was Alexander Lord Gordon, son and heir of George 4th Earl of Huntley. The Peerage writers, on the other hand, say she was the second daughter, Lady Margaret, and state that Lady Barbara was married to James Lord Fleming, ancestor of the Earls of Wigton. In 1549, the name of Lord Fleming is not once mentioned, nor while the Duke of Chatellerault was Governor.

After carefully examining the matter, I think these contradictory statements may be thus explained.

Alexander Lord Gordon, who was married in 1549, died during his father's life, without issue, and his next brother, George, became heir-apparent before April, 1553, as we find him styled in Charters of that date George Lord Gordon. He also married a daughter, the Lady Anne Hamilton, in 1558; and four years later he succeeded to the Earldom of Huntley. He died in May, 1576.

James, fourth Lord Fleming who succeeded his father in 1547, on the 21st of December, 12th year of Mary [1554], granted by Charter under the Great Seal part of the Barony of Lenzie in favour of Lady Barbara Hamilton, his spouse. He was then a youth, not twenty years of age. Five years later this lady was again a widow, Lord Fleming being one of the three deputies sent to France, who died prematurely on their return in December, 1558, not without strong suspicions of having been poisoned. He left one daughter, who afterwards married for her first husband Sir John Maitland Lord Thirlestone, High Chancellor of Scotland.—*D. L.*

In these *Minor Poems* Lauder appears as a sterner and more earnest Reformer than in his *Office and Dewtie of Kyngis* written thirteen years before; and our estimate of him must rise accordingly. The *Office*, printed in 1556, was 'laitlie compylit be' him. We may fairly ask 'what in that year, or the years just before, should have made our Poet think specially of this theme; what Kyng or Ruler in his own land he wished to advise,—for he could hardly hope that his words would reach any other than Scotch ears—?' Works like the *Office* are generally called out by some special occasion :—compare

he advice to the 'kingis of tender age' (p. 49, line 1658) in the
Lancelot of the Laik, edited for us by Mr Skeat, which he shows was
probably meant for the young James III., ab. 1478 A.D.; and as
Lauder had a special cause for writing his *Minor Poems*, so I believe
that he had one for writing the *Office*. In 1554, Mary of Guise, the
French mother of the infant Queen, not yet thirteen, was made
Regent of Scotland. Her misrule of the land was to be great, though
of her "it was justly said that her talents and virtues were her
own; her errors and faults the effect of her deference to the advice
of others, and especially of her aspiring brothers."[1] Her first act
almost was,

The Queene chaunged al the Officers, & made the Earle of
Cassels thresorer, and Veilmort a Frenchman Controller; also an
other Frenchman called Monsieur Rubie, keeper of the great seale,
in place of the Earle of Huntley, who was Chauncellour, and then in
warde. These mens counsell, and Monsieur Doysels, she vsed prin-
cipally in al things. (Holinshed, *The Hystorie of Scotland*, i. 482,
col. 2, ed. 1577.)

Mary of Guise was a strong Papist; she was to try, at least, to
persecute the Protestants, and for that end to plunge Scotland into
the civil war, from the troubles of which and her own dropsical dis-
order she died in 1560. Coming events cast their shadows before.
In 1555 and 1556, Lauder might well have seen special reason, in
the temper of Mary of Guise and her advisers, to think and to write
'On the Office and Dewtie of Kyngis', as well as that of 'Spirituall
Pastoris and Temporall Iugis'.

After that, he wrote for Queen Mary's first marriage in the summer of 1558,—when she was but sixteen,—a Play (Mr D. Laing's
biography, *Office*, p. vii.). Then came the Reformation in 1560, the
beautiful young widowed Queen's return to Scotland in 1561 (Aug.
19), and her second marriage, on the 29th of July, 1565, with the
handsome, dissolute, vicious, and passionate Darnley, who was thereupon proclaimed King of Scotland. It would have been well for
Darnley had he pondered over Lauder's warning on 'quhat sall
becum to kyngis that contynewis in Iniquitie, and neclectis thair
offices,' how

[1] Sir W. Scott's *Hist. of Scotland*, ii. 65.

> '3our vitious lyfe, and couatyce,
> And the abusyng of 3our offyce,
> Vsand 3our fleschelie vane plesuris
> Oppressand 3our pure creaturis,
> And 3our fals glosing of the wrang,
> Sall nocht mak 3ow to rax heir lang.'
> *Office*, p. 7, l. 127-132.

His strangled corpse in the garden near the Kirk of Field[1] on Sunday night, the 9th of February, 1567, need not then have turned Lauder's words into a prophecy; a prophecy fulfilled again in Mary's own abdication five months afterwards. Her infant son, little more than a year old, was crowned at Stirling on the 29th of July, 1567.

Well, the dissolute Darnley's accomplices murder her favourite Rizzio in Mary's presence. A few hours after she has left her husband, he is murdered, and his house is blown into the air—undoubtedly, I think, with her connivance [2]—by the hirelings of a greater—and an ugly—brute, whom she marries, after he has, to secure her, divorced his own wife. Mary's abdication follows; her imprisonment too; civil war breaks out; famine and pestilence ravage the land; selfishness and self-seeking abound; and at last Lauder speaks,—not to kings, but to People; not to point the moral of his earlier work; facts did that;—but because of the social wrongs around him, of ' the miserabill estait of this present world;

> This warld is war nor euer it was !
> Full of myscheif and all malice ! . . . .
> How lang, Lorde, sall this warld indure?

In 1568 there was enough in the political condition of Scotland to make any patriot raise his voice. What especially was there in the social and moral state of the country to make it needful for a faithful Minister of the Word of God to speak out?

First, Famine; secondly, Plague, says Chambers's *Domestic Annals of Scotland*, both of which called forth a hellish display of the greed and selfishness of the rich, and not only made Lauder

---

[1] The name of the Church near which was the house in which Darnley was blown up by Bothwell and his men.

[2] See J. Hill Burton's *History of Scotland*, iv. 344-5, ed. 1868.

indignant, but good Dr Gilbert Skeyne sad. First, then, of the Famine:

"1567-8. In consequence of an extremely dry summer, the yield of grain and herbage in 1567 was exceedingly defective. The ensuing winter being unusually severe, there was a sad failure of the means of supporting the domestic animals. A stone of hay came to be sold in Derbyshire at 5*d*. (*Holinshed's Chronicle*), which seems to have been regarded as a starvation price. There was a general mortality among the sheep and horses. In Scotland, the opening of 1568 was marked by scarcity and all its attendant evils.

'There was,' says a contemporary chronicler (*Historie of King James the Sext*, 1825), 'exceeding dearth of cornes, in respect of the penury thereof in the land, and that beforehand a great quantity thereof was transported to other kingdoms: for remeed whereof inhibitions were made sae far out of season, that nae victual should be transported furth of the country under the pain of confiscation, even then when there was no more left either to satisfy the indigent people, or to plenish the ordinar mercats of the country as appertenit.'"

[1] 'For the entres of the next ʒeir, 1568, thair was exceeding dearth of cornes in respect of scant in the countrey, that so mikle was transportit to other kingdomes: for remeid quhairoff, inhibitions were maid so farr out of season, that na victuall should be transportit out of the contrie under the paine of confiscatioun: even quhen thair was na mair ather to satisfie the people, or to plenishe the common mercattis of the countrie as appertenit.' *The Historie of King James the Sext*. Ed. M. L[aing.] Edinburgh, 1804, p. 33-4.

Let the reader now turn to lines 456-497 of Lauder's *Godlie Tractate*, p. 17-19 below, and see what he says of this Dearth, and how he lashes the greedy rich who let the poor die without mercy, while they, every fat Sow of them, feed and flatter one another:[2]

¶ ʒour gredynes, it stink*is* and fylis the air! 468
I vg[3] ʒour Murthour and Hirschip[4] to declair!
For thocht ʒe sla nocht pure men with ʒour knyues,
ʒit with ʒour dearth ʒe tak from thame the lyues.

---

[1] As the first published copy varies a little from the other, I give it in a second column.
[2] See too p. 26, l. 9-12.   [3] shudder, loathe.
[4] harrying, plundering.

¶ Quhat differs dearth frome creuell briganrye, 472
Quhen that ȝe mak the Pure for hunger dye ?
No thing at all, most trewlie to conclude,
Except of thame ȝe do nocht draw the blude,
For ȝe contryne¹ thame,—as wyse me*n* merk*is* and seis,—
Till one of thir two grit Extremiteis ;
Till vtter hirschip,² with bying of thair fude ;
And want tha money ? than schortlie to conclude,
Thair is no credeit, bot of Necessitie, 480
The Pure Broder, for Hunger he man die.

¶ God send ȝow nocht *th*e Uictall of the ground
That ȝe the pepill suld Fameis and confound ;
Bot that ȝe sould thair-of gude Stewarts be, 484
Helpand the Pure in thair necessite.
¶ Wo be till him that hurdis vp his Corne,
Syne kepis it vp to dearth, fra morne to morne ³ !
Bot Gods blissing sall lycht vpon his head, 488
That lat*is* it furth, that pure men may get bread.
¶ Bot as ȝe cloise ȝour Girnall*is* frome *th*e puris,
Quhilk*is* now thairby grit miserie induris,
So God sall cloise on ȝow, for ȝour grit Sin, 492
His Heauinlie Porte, quhe*n that* ȝe wald faine cum in.
¶ So on this wyse quhe*n that* ȝe scurge the pure,
God sall ȝow Plaig agane for that, be sure !

Secondly, on the people thus weakened by want, fell the Plague.

"In 1568, Edinburgh and other parts of the country suffered grievously from the plague :
'The plague beginning to rage in Edinburgh, in a dreadful and destructive manner, the following Regulations and Orders were made by the Council, to prevent its spreading.'
"These 'Statuts for the Baillies of the Mure and ordering of the Pest' you will find in Maitland's *History of Edinburgh*, p. 31, etc."
(D. Laing.)

Here, too, Chambers helps us by his extracts from the *Diurnal* and Dr Skeyne, and his account of the measures taken in Edinburgh to stay the plague, for which the reader must refer to the *Domestic*

---

¹ ? *Contraindre*, constrain ; or, 'contrive.'
² scarcity, want. (As the effect of devastation. *Jamieson*.)
³ The modern Political-Economy defence of the hoarders is all very well when you have a proper Poor-Law, though there are limits to the doctrine even then ; but when you've nothing that can be called a Poor-Law, as in 1568 (see Sir G. Nicholls's *Hist. of the Scotch Poor-Law*), matters are altered.

nnals, or *Maitland*, as above. The extracts from Skeyne I enlarge, as I like the man.

1568, Sep. 8. 'Ane called James Dalgliesh, merchant, brought the pest int[o] Edinburgh.'—*Diurnal of Remarkable Occurrents in Scotland*, 1513-75 (Maitland Club, 4to. 1833).

[1] 'Sen it hes plesit the inscrutabill Consall and Iustice of God, Beneuolent readar) that this present plaig and maist detestabil iseise of Pest, be laitlie enterit in this Realme, it becummis euerie ne in his awin vocatione to be not only most studious, be perfecioun of lyfe, to mitigat apperandlie the iuste wrathe of God touart s, in this miserable tyme : Bot also to be maist curagius in suffering f trauail, for the aduancement of the commoun weilth. I, beand nouit in that part, *seand the pure of Christ inlaik*,[2] *without assistance of support in bodie, al men detestand aspectioun, speche, or comnunicatioun with thame*, thoucht expedient to put schortlie in wryte as it hes plesit God to supporte my sober knawlege) quhat becummis euerie ane baith for preseruatioun and cure of sic diseise, quhairin (gude readar) thou sall nather abyde greit eruditioun nor eloquence, bot onlie the sentence and iugement of the maist ancient writaris in medicine expressit in vulgar langage without poleit or affectionat termis.'

The second passage in which Skeyne speaks of the cruel neglect of the poor by the rich is at the end of his treatise. After he has old people that the advice of Physicians is necessary, because every one is blinder than the mole in such things as concern their own health,[3] he adds,

'And besyde that, euerie ane is becum sa detestable to vther (quhilk is to lamentit). *And speciallie the pure in sicht of the riche, as gif thay var not equall with thame twichand thair Creatioun, bot rather without saule or spirite, as beistis degenerat fra mankynd.* Quhairfoir lat vs hvmble our selfis in presence of our God and Father of all consolatioun, that be the intercessioun of Iesus Christ our Saluiour, and of his mercy & grace, he will indue vs with the

---

[1] *Skeyne's Tracts, Bannatyne Club*: 'To the Readar.'
[2] want, (and thence, as here,) perish.
[3] 'Considerand alwayis as thair is diuersite of tyme, cuntray, aige and consuetude to be obseruit in tyme of ministratioun of ony medicine preseruatiue or curatiue, ewin sa thair is diuers kyndis of pest, quhilkis may be eisely knawin and diuidit be weil lernit Phisicianis, quhais conseill in tyme of sic dangeir of lyfe is baith profitable and necessar, in respect that in this pestienciall diseis euerie ane is mair blind nor the Moudeuart [mole] in sic thingis as concernis thair awin helth.'—p. 44, *Skeyne's Tracts, Bannatyne Club*.

spreit of repentance, that vnfenȝeitlie we may conuerte vs vnto him, reformand our deprauat and corrupt leuing in tymis by past; And also apply ourselfis in tymis cumming, to the obedience of his Godly will and obseruing of his commandementis, that thairby he may not onlie remoue sic punischment and Plaig frome vs, Bot also that baith riche and puir may leue in sic Godly and ciuill societie, as may be agreable to his godlie will, that finallie we may be participant of his kingdome preparit for his Electe fra the beginning.'

The good Doctor gives plenty of directions and prescriptions how to treat the plague, but, as above seen, his first call is to repentance :—

'The principal preseruatiue cure of the pest, is, to return to God, quha is maist puissant, with ane affectionat and ardent will and hart, to imploir the support of his Maiestie, be the intercessioun of his deir Sone Iesus Christ, to pacifie his wrathe aganis vs, takand away sic punischement: and as he hes saifit vs fra eternall deithe, so he wald saif vs fra sick corporall dethe, quhilk iustlie for oure demeritis persecutis vs. Thairfor, not pretermittand sic support as it hes plesit his Godlie will to schaw vs, be guid succes of dew prescriptioun of nature, be quhilk meanis reasone prescryuis preseruatioun to consist in twa thingis: first to prepair the bodie apte to purgatioun: Secundly to mak it quhilk may offend debile in actione or impressioun[1].'—(*Skeyne's Tracts*, p. 17.)

"This pestilence," says Chambers (*Dom. Ann.* i. 55), "lasting till February [156$\frac{8}{9}$], is said to have carried off 2500 persons in Edinburgh, which could not be much less than a tenth of the population."

Before we quit the Plague, let us notice that during it, one George Bannatyne, a Scotch lawyer's son, retired alone—not like Boccaccio's feigned ten (seven fair ladies, and three lovers of some of them) to their country-house, near Florence, for ten days, during the terrible Black Plague of 1348—into the country, and there for three months copied into his *Ballat Buik* '372 poems covering no less than 800 folio pages.'[2] It's an ill wind that blows nobody good.

---

[1] Under Nov. 18, 1568, Chambers says, "In this time of dearth and pestilence, the council of the Canongate providently ordained that 'the fourpenny loaf be weel baken and dried, gude and sufficient stuff, and keep the measures and paik [stroke] of twenty-two ounces;' 'that nae browsters nor ony tapsters, sell ony dearer ale nor 6*d*. the pint;' and 'that nae venters of wine buy nae new wine dearer than that they may sell the same commonly to all our sovereign's lieges for 16*d*. the pint.'"—*Dom. Ann.* i. 58.

[2] *Domestic Annals*, i. 58: "A pleasing memorial of this visitation remains in the Manuscript Collections of George Bannatyne, after three months' labour,

On the Harlotry of which Lauder complains in his *Godlie Tractate*, p. 19,

> ¶ I neid nocht rekkin ȝour filthye Harlotrie:
> It is so knawin, our alquhair, oppinlie;
> Quhilk to rehearse, It mak[i]s me abhor,   500

and to dissuade men from which, he wrote a separate poem, the *Gude Exempill*, p. 38, below, we may compare the following article from the General Assembly of the Kirk and Nobles, &c., to the Queen in 1565, printed in Knox's Works, vol. ii., p. 486:

> 'Fifthly, That such horrible crimes as now abound within this Realme, without any correction, to the great contempt of God and his Word; such as Idolatry, blasphemie of God's name, manifest breaking of the Sabbath-day, witchcraft, sorcery, inchantment, *adultery, manifest whoredome, maintenance of bordals*, murther, slaughter, oppression, with many other detestable crimes, may be severely punished; and Judges appointed in every province and diocese, for execution thereof, with power to do the same and that by Act of Parliament.'—*Articles of the General Assembly met in Edinburgh on the 25th June*, 1565.

Going back three years earlier, we find another complaint of the Kirk, which we may quote, not only because it dwells on the general vices of the people, but also touches the superstition of the Mass, and the debauched lives of the Romish clergy, on which Lauder dwells on p. 13 of his Godlie Tractate, and which Lyndesay lashed so bitterly in his *Satyre*, p. 422-3, 452, 481, 498 (on Prelates' daughters, &c., 518, 523), 504-6, 517, 534, 538, &c. of the Society's edition. The complaint also notices the sad state of the poor labourers, and the iniquitous cheating of the poor Ministers by the nobles, who kept back their scanty salaries and made them live a beggar's life, a subject to which we shall return below (p. xx.).

In 'The Supplication of the Assemblye of the Kyrk,' 29 June, 1562, to the Queen and her Privy Council, *Knox's Works*, ii. 338-41, the Assembly say:

—and hard work it must have been,—as appears from the Valedictory Address at the end of the Preface:

> 'The Writtar to the Readare.
> Heir endis this Buik, writtin in tyme of pest,
> Quhen we fra labor was compeld to rest,
> In to the thre last moneths of this yeir, &c.' [1568]."—D. Laing.

'that your Grace and Counsall may understand what be the thingis we desyre to be reformed, we will begyn at that quhilk we assuredlie know to be the fontane and spring of all other evillis that now abound in this Realme, to wit, That idoll and bastard service of God, the Messe; the fontane, we call it, of all impietie, not only becaus that many tack boldnes to syn be reassone of the opinioun which thei have conceaved of that idoll, to wit, That by the vertew of it, thei get remissioun of thair synnes; but also becaus that under the cullour of the Messe, are hoores, adulteraris, drunkardis, blasphemaris of God, of His holy Word and Sacramentis, and such other manifest malefactouris, manteaned and defended: for lett any Messe-sayare, or earnest manteanar thairof, be deprehended in any of the foirnamed crymes, no executioun can be had, for all is done in haiterent of his religioun; and so are wicked men permitted to live wickedlie, clocked and defended by that odious idoll.'

<small>This causes the Quenis religioun to have many favouraris.</small>

'The Secound that we requyre, is punishement of horrible vices, sic as ar *adultery, fornicatioun, open hurdome*, blasphemye, contempt of God, of his Word, and Sacramentis; quhilkis in this Realme, for lack of punishement, do evin now so abound, that syne is reputed to be no syne. And tharfoir, as that we see the present signes of Goddis wrath now manifestlie appear, so do we foirwarne, that he will stryck, or it be long, yf his law without punishement be permitted thus manifestlie to be contempned. Yf any object, that punishementis can nott be commanded to be executed without a Parliament; We answer that the eternall God in his Parliament has pronounced death to be the punishement for adulterye and for blasphemye; whose actis yf ye putt not to executioun (seing that kingis are but his lieutennentis, having no power to geve lyefe, whair he commandis death,) as that he will reputt you, and all otheris that foster vice, patronis of impietie, so will he nott faill to punishe you for neglecting of his judgementis.

<small>Grudgeing of the nobilitie one against other.</small>

Our Third requeast concerneth the Poore, who be of thre sortis: the poore lauboraris of the ground; the poore desolat beggaris, orphelyns, wedoes, and strangaris; and the poore ministeris of Christ Jesus, his holie evangell, quhilk ar all so crewallie entreated by this last pretended Ordour tacken for sustentatioun of Ministeris, that thair latter miserie far surmonteth the formar. For now the poore lauboraris of the ground ar so oppressed by the creualtie of those that pay thair Thrid, that they for the most parte advance upoun the poore, whatsoever they pay to the Quene, or to any other. As for the verray indigent and poore, to whome God commandis a sustentatioun to be provided of the Teyndis, they ar so dyspised, that it is a wonder that the sone geveth heat and lycht to the earth, whair Godis name is so frequentlie called upoun, and no mercy (according to his commandiment) schawin to his creaturis. And also for the

Ministeris, thair lyvingis ar so appointed, that the most parte shall lyye but a beggaris lyef. And all cumeth of that impietie, that the idill bellies of Christis ennemyes mon be fedd in thair formare delicacie.'

Against these, and other vices that Lauder denounced, his threat, as he wrote, was being fulfilled, though the poor, as usual, got most of the punishment that ought to have fallen on the rich :

<pre>
For Disobedience vnto Gods wourd,   628
ȝe sall be Plagit with Hunger, Pest, and swourd,
With Hirschip, Fyre, with Dearth, and Pestelence,
Because ȝe Sin aganis ȝour Conscience ; (Godlie Tractate, p. 22) ;
</pre>

and the scenes around him justify his outcry in his *Lamentatioun* :

<pre>
¶ For to behauld this Miserie,
    My breist in baill it dois combure ;
 Sen reuth is none, nor ȝit Pitie,
    How lang, Lord, wyll this warld indure ?   84
</pre>

As a proof that the evils of which Lauder complains were of some standing, we may quote from the very striking and socially-valuable poem of Alexander Scott, 'Ane New-Yeir Gift to the Quene Mary, quhen scho come first hame,' 1561. The coincidence is marked of the lines in italics below, and the 'Works to agree with Words' (*Godlie Tractate*, p. 23), the 'Gredie Idole Averice' (*ib.* p. 20, l. 547), 'Couatyce a worse Idol than the Mass' (p. 21-2, l. 601-2), the grasping Landlords, the Labourers and Tenants turned out of their holdings (*ib.* p. 19-20, l. 528-536).

<pre>
¹' As Beis tak Wax and Honey of the Floure,
     So does the Faithful of God's Word tak Fruit ;
   As Wasps receive frae aff the same but sour,
     Sae Reprobates the Scripture dois rebute,
</pre>

¹ pp. 8—11 *of Ramsay's Evergreen* ('Leicester to Mary'). This bad copy having been set before I knew of Mr David Laing's excellent edition of Alexander Scott's Works from George Bannatyne's MS, 1568 A.D., I add Mr Laing's text here ;—Scott is a man we ought to know more of in England :—

<pre>
         As bèis takkis walx and honye of the floure,
           So dois the faythfull of Goddis word tak frute ;
         As waspis ressauis of the same bot soure,
           So reprobatis Christis buke dois rebute :
</pre>

Words without Warks availeth not a Cute,
To seis thy Subjects sae in Luve and Feir,
  That Richt and Reason in thy Realm m[a]y rute,
God give thee Grace agains this gude new ʒeir!
' The Epistles and Evangells now are Preicht,
  Bot Sophestrie or Ceremonys vain;
Thy People, maist Part, truely now are teicht
  To put away Idolatrie prophane;
  But in sum Hearts is graven new again,
An Image callit cursd Covetice of Geir;
  Now to expell that Idol stands up plain,
God give thee Grace agains this gude new ʒeir!
' For Sum are sene at Sermons, sum sa haly,
  Singand Sanct David's Psalter on their Buiks,
And are but Biblists fairsing full their Belly,
  Backbytand Nybours, noying them in Nuiks,
  Ruggand and reivand up Kirk Rents lyke Rukes;
Lyke very Wasps against God's Word mak Weir;
  Now sic Christians to kiss with Chanters Kirks,
God give thee Grace agains this gude new ʒeir!
' Dewtie and Detts are driven by Doubleness,
  And Folks are flemit frae ʒung Faith Professors,
The greatest ay the greidyar, I gess,
  To plant quhere Preists and Parsons were Possessors.

Wordis, without werkis, availʒeis nocht a cute:
To seiss thy subiectis so in luf and feir,
  That rycht and reasoun in thy realme may rute,
God gife thé grace aganis this gude new-ʒeir.

The epistollis and evangelis now ar prechit,
  But sophistrie or ceremoneis vaine;
Thy pepill, maist pairt, trewlie now ar techit,
  To put away Idolatrie prophaine:
  Bot in sum hartis is gravit new agane,
Ane Image, callit cuvatyce of geir;
  Now, to expell that idoll standis vp plane,
God gif thé grace aganis this gude new-ʒeir.

For sum quhen sene at sermonis seme sa halye,
  Singand Sanct *Dauidis* psalter on thair bukis,
And ar bot biblistis fairsing full thair bellie,
  Bakbytand nychtbouris noyand thame in nwikis,
  Ruging and raisand vp kirk-rentis lyke ruikis;
As werrie waspis aganis Goddis word makis weir:
  Sic Christianis to kiss with chanteris kuikis,
God gife thé grace aganis this gude new-ʒeir.

Dewtie and dettis ar drevin by dowbilnes,
  Auld folkis ar flemit fra ʒung fayth professouris,
The grittest ay, the greddiar I gess,
  To plant quhair preistis and personis wer possessouris;

Teinds are uptane by Testament Transgressors.
Credence is past of Promise, thocht they sweir,
  To punish Palmers, and reproach Oppressors,
God give thee Grace agains this gude new ʒeir!

' Puir Folk are famist with their Fassions new,
  They fail for Falt that had before at fouth,
Leil Labourers lament and Tennants trew,
  That they ar hurt and herriet North and South,
The Heidsmen have " *Cor mundum* " in their Mouth,
But nevir mynd to give the Man his Meir,
  To quench thir quent Calamities so cowth,
God give thee Grace agains this gude new ʒeir!

' Protestands tak the Friers auld Antetewme
  Ready Resavers, but to render nocht,
So *Lairds uplift Men's Leiving*, ower thy Rewme,
  And are richt crabit quhen they crave them ocht[1]:
Be they unpaid, thy Pursevants are socht,
To pund pure Commons Corn and Cattle keir,
  To vissy all thir wrangous Warks are wrocht,
God give thee Grace agains the gude new ʒeir!'

On the Sorcery that Lauder denounces in his *Lamentatioun*, l. 33-36, p. 27 below, we need only refer to the many witch-trials of the period, and may quote two passages from Knox's *Fourt Book of*

> Teindis ar vptane be testament transgressouris;
> Credence is past, off promeiss thoc*h*t thaj sweir:
>   To punisch Papistis and reproche oppressouris,
> God gif th*é* grace aganis t*h*is gude new-ʒeir.
>
> Pure folk ar famist wit*h* t*h*ir fassionis new,
>   Thaj faill for falt t*h*at had befoir at fouth;
> Leill labouraris lamentis, and tennentis trew,
>   That t*h*aj ar hurt, and hareit north and south:
> The heidismen hes "*cor mundum*" in t*h*air mouth,
> Bot nevir wit*h* mynd to gif *the* man his meir:
>   To quenche thir quent calamiteis so cowth,
> God gife th*é* grace aganis t*h*is gude new-ʒeir.
>
> Protestandis takis t*h*e freiris auld antetewme,
>   Reddie ressauaris bot to rander nocht;
> So lairdis vpliftis mennis leifing ouir thy rewme,
>   And ar rycht crabit quhen thaj crave t*h*ame ocht,
> Be thaj vnpayit, thy pursevandis ar socht,
> To pund pure communis corne and cattell keir:
>   To wisy all t*h*ir wrangus workis ar wrocht,
> God gife th*é* grace againis t*h*is gude new-ʒeir.
> D. Laing's edition (1821) of Alex. Scott's Poems, pp. 8—10, ll. 105—152.

[1] See Lyndesay's *Satyre*, p. 474, lines 2567-77.

the Progresse and Continuance of Treu Religioun within Scotland (Works, ii. 391), under the year 1563 : "Justice-Courtis war halden, thevis and murtheraris war punished ; *twa witches war burnt;* the eldest was so blynded with the Devill, that sche affirmed, ' That ne Judge had power ower hir.'" Also, p. 357 :

'The Erle [of Huntley] immediatlie after his tacken, departed this lyiff without any wound, or yitt appearance of any strock, whair of death might have enseued ; and so, becaus it was laitt, he was cassen over-thorte a pair of crealles, and so was caryed to Abirdene, and was laid in the Tolbuyth thairof, that *the response whiche hi: wyffis wyttches had gevin* mycht be fulfilled, whay all affirmed (as the most parte say) that that same nycht should he be in the Tolbuytl of Abirdene without any wound upoun his body. When his Lady gatt knowledge thairof, sche blamed *hir principale witche callec Janet;* but sche stoutlie defended hir self, (as the devill can eve do), and affirmed that she geve a trew answer, albeit she spack not all the treuth ; for she knew that he should be thair dead : but tha could nott proffeit my Lady. Scho was angrye and sorye for a seassone but the Devill, the Messe, and *wyttches* have als great credyte of hi this day as thei had sevin yearis ago.'

Another point that evidently came home to Lauder, was th scornful treatment of 'virtewus men that laketh Ryches' (p. 36) He, no doubt, had found himself, and seen others of the able godl men around him, scorned and snubbed by the rich of his time, not allowed to defile the floor of dainty dames (p. 28, 1. 57), thrust aside to make room for a rich idiot, a blunt bubo, a beast with bags (p. 36-7), or a flatterer, bragger, or brothel-haunter. As Knox said in his Sermon vpon Sonday the 19 of August 1565, for the which he 'was inhibite preaching for a season' (leaf 14, back, ed. 1566) :

" Now haue the wicked their counsels, their thrones, & finally, handeling for the most part of al things that are vpon the face of the earth; but the pore seruants of God are reputed *vnworthy oj mens prescnce;* yea, they are *more vile* before these proude tyraunts, *than is very dirt and mire that is troden vnder fote.*"

'Money before Morals' was Society's motto then, as now; and our Reformer was right in denouncing it. Lauder had seen witl his own eyes, as he tells us (p. 13, 1. 319, below), Popish Cardina : as companions of Scottish Kings : they, corrupt in doctrine, in pure in life, oppressors of the poor, as Lyndesay shows in h

Satyre. He now saw his own fellows, pure in doctrine, pure in life, helpers of the poor, treated like beggars by the mere rich. And he rightly told these snobs that God would punish them for their baseness.

The rascally plunder of Church-property by the Scotch nobles—"couetous clawbaks of the new court," Knox calls some in his Preface to the Sermon just quoted,—which we have already noticed, p. xv. above, had left the Ministers poor. Parliament had decreed, says Sir Walter Scott, in his *History of Scotland*, ii. 72,

"that the church property, whether in the hands of the bishops or of lay titulars,—as the lay impropriators were called,—should be liable to be taxed to the extent of one third of their amount, for the support of the Protestant clergy; and a committee was appointed to *modify*, as it was called, the especial stipends payable in every individual case, reserving by far the greatest proportion of the fund in reversion to the prelatic possessor or lay titular. The obvious selfishness of these enactments give just offence to the clergy. John Knox, deeply incensed at the avarice of the nobility, pronounced from the pulpit of Edinburgh, that two parts of the Church revenue were bestowed on the devil, and a third divided between God and the devil. A hundred marks Scottish (not six pounds sterling) was the usual allowance *modified* to the minister of a parish: some parishes were endowed with a stipend of thrice that amount; and the whole sum allowed for the maintenance of the National Church, consisting of a thousand parishes, was about three thousand five hundred pounds a year, which paltry endowments were besides irregularly paid, and very much begrudged. When it is considered how liberal the ancient kings and governors of Scotland had been to the Church of Rome, it appears that in this point, as of all others in doctrine and discipline, the Scottish Reformers had held a line of conduct diametrically opposite to that pursued by their Catholic ancestors. This unkindly parsimony towards themselves was the more acutely felt by the Protestant preachers, as the principal lords of the congregation, and the lord James of St Andrew's himself, were the persons by whom these miserable stipends were *modified*. 'Who would have thought,' said the ardent Knox, 'that when Joseph ruled in Egypt, his brethren would have come down thither for corn, and returned with their sacks empty? Men would have thought that Pharaoh's storehouse would have been emptied ere the sons of Jacob were placed in risk of starving for hunger.' Wisheart of Pittarrow, a zealous reformer, was appointed Comptroller, to levy and pay the allotted stipends; but as the poor Ministers complained to heaven and earth that they were not able to obtain payment even of the small pittance allowed them, it became a common phrase to bless the good laird of Pittarrow as a sincere professor, but bid the devil receive the Comptroller as a greedy extortioner." [1]

We may also hear, as to the scanty provision for the poor Ministers, the Address of

"The Superintendents, Ministers, and Commissioners of the Churches reformed within this realme of Scotlande, assembled in Edenbrough the .xxv. daye of December .1565. to all faithfull within the same realme, desire grace and peace, from God the Father, and from our Lorde Iesus Christ, with the perpetual comfort of the holye Ghost."—p. 1.

"The sorrowfull complayntes of all ministers in generall, and of some nowe more to be lamented in others in particuler, being considered in this oure last assembly (beloued in the Lord Iesus), diuers men were of diuers iudgementes, howe the griefe and pouertie of such as faithfully trauayle in their vocation within the Church of God somewhat might be relieued."—pp. 1, 2.

"With what conscience can we eate oure owne bread, and know the bowels of such as offers to vs the breade of lyfe, and minister to vs spirituall things, to craue of God and vs but a reasonable sustentation; and yet can not finde suche fauour at oure handes, as Turkes finde amongest Turkes, and Iewes amongest that blinded nation."—p. 3.

"Now if we think that none within Scotlande lackes true faith, yea, if we thinke that our children can attayne to the right knowledge of God without true doctrine, then maye we dreame with our selues, that ministers are not necessarie, and so are we nothing addicted vnto them? But if that faith commeth by hearing .... of God's worde, and that God's word is not sent vnto vs absolutely from heauen by Aungels, but is planted by the holy spirite in the heartes and mouthes of men whome God of his mercye sendes forth into the world, to sowe therin the seede of his Euangell, we can not but confesse our selues detters to our ministers. The dispisers of whome, yea all suche as to their power supporte them not in their necessities, are before his throne iudged contempners of his owne maiestie. And therfore yet once againe, let euery faithfull [2] consider what is his duetie, and let vs abhor that ingratitude that we shuld suffer *the seruants of the Lorde Iesus to begge, or trauaile in pouerty before our eyes*, for if we doe, we banishe from vs Iesus Christ and the light of his euangell."—pp. 8, 9.

Many a fatt Souch's [3] descendants still feed on the plunder of the

---

[1] As to the smallness of Ministers' stipends, see too *Knox's Works*, ii. p 311, 312, 340, 342, 383, 470, 485, 489, and that they could not get them paid, ii. 511, 517.

[2] faithful person.   [3] p. 17, l. 460; p. 26, l. 9.

poor Ministers, while the successors of Lauder and his worthy fellows have little more, comparatively, than the beggarly pittances of old.

The 'prophane Monstruus hose' of which Lauder speaks, p. 17, l. 425, were doubtless those described by Stubbes as worn in England in and before 1583:

"The gally-hosen are made very large and wide, reaching downe to their knees onely, with three or foure guardes a peece, laid down along either hose. And the Venetian hosen, they reach beneath the knee to the gartering place of the leg, where they are tyed finely with silk points, or some such like, and laied on also with rewes of lace, or gardes, as the other before. And yet notwithstanding, all this is not sufficient, except they be made of silk, velvet, saten, damask, and other such precious things besides... In times past, kings ... would not disdaine to weare a paire of hosen <small>The great excesse</small> of a noble, tenne shillinges, or a marke, price, with all <small>used in hosen.</small> the rest of their apparel after the same rate; but now it is a small matter to bestowe twentie nobles, ten pound, *twentie pound, fortie pound, yea, a hundred pound, of one paire of breeches.* (God be mercifull unto us!) . . . ." p. 58, *Collier's Reprint,* 1869.

See on this point Fairholt's *Costume in England,* p. 208-213, with the cuts and quotations he gives, including part of that above from Stubbes. These 'monstruus' breeches[1] were stuft with wool, flax, and hair—as the ballad 'A lamentable Complaint of the Countreymen for the Loss of their Cattelles Tails' tells (*Fairholt,* p. 211).

On the Martyrs in Lauder's days,—whom he says (*Godlie Tractate,* p. 24, l. 676-81) he saw suffer patiently most cruel death, and yet might have had life, wife, and bairns, if they'd have refused the Word of God—we cannot do better than take a few passages from his contemporary, Henry Charteris's, Preface to Sir David Lyndesay's *Warkis,* published in the same year as Lauder's own *Tractate,* 1568. Charteris, asking why the Papist Prelates, whose vices and ignorance Lyndesay so openly and wittily exposed, have not been able to get hold of him and burn him, says:

Sum will think because he was continuallie in Court, and seruit the King, he was esilie ouersene. Bot in my iugement, that is the

---

[1] Compare too, in 1598, *A Health to the Gentlemanly profession of Seruingmen,* p. 138 (ed. 1868, Roxburghe Library): "Northeren Carsies are not now weareable in Breetches, for it will shrinke, and the fashion is now to haue Venetians of the largest size: yf they will not holde a bushell a breetch, they are not saleable in Birtchen lane."

greiter cause of offence : namelie to haif thair vaniteis and wickitnes publischit in Court, and sicht of Princis. Nouther culd this be saiftie to vtheris ; M. Patrik Hammiltou*n*, Abbot of Feirn, being of the blude Royall, being ane man of greit literature, and of sic lyfe that the verray enemeis thame selfis war enforcit to commend and allow him, ʒit did he nocht eschaip thair malice, bot sufferit cruell deith be fyre. Robert Forester, alswa gentilman, on the samin maner was tormentit.

Again, after instancing the Martyrdoms in England and abroad, Charteris says :

Now our Prelates laith to ly behind, willing to schaw *th*air gude seruice to *th*e halie Sait, apprehe*n*dit heir in Scotland, Paull Craw, teiching the doctrine quhilk Uicleif & Hus had teichit, & maid ane Sacrifice of him in Sanctandrois. And findand the sawour of this Sacrifice fragrant and smelland, thay tuke the Uicar of Dolour, Freir Kelour, Symsone, Bawerage, Kennedie, Stratoun, Gourlay, and mony ma, quha, because *th*ai culd not allow *th*air vaine superstitiones and Idolatries, expres aganis the co*m*mandeme*n*t of *th*e Lord thair God, war cuttit of be the fyre. Thay had now lernit to dispute with fyre & faggot ; for our auld Bischoppis & Pastouris war decayit, quhilkis war wo*n*t to be lampis, and as it war leidsternis, to all nationis adiace*n*t.

A little further on, Charteris adds :

And yit ane lytill befoir his [Lyndesay's] deith thay brint M. George Uischart[1], and Adam Wallace, Mariner. And schortlie efter our Authouris deith thay tuke the auld ma*n* Walter Mill, and cruellie brint him : althocht fra that fyre rais sic ane stew, quhilk struke sic sturt to thair stemokis, that thay rewit it euer efter.

On the general evils in Scotland in 1568, Charteris says :

And gif he [Lyndesay] had leifit in *th*ir lait dayis, quhat had he said of *th*e vnnatural murtheris : *th*e cruel slauchteris : *th*e manifest reiffis : *th*e continuall heirschippis : *th*e plane oppressionis : *th*e lytill regard of all persones to *th*e co*m*moun weilth : *th*e mantening of derth, to the vniuersall hurt of the pure in transporting of victuallis furth of

---

[1] 1545. In the Lent season the Cardinall of S. Andrewes caused al the Bishoppes and Prelates of the Realme to assemble at the towne of S. Andrewes, where a learned man, named M. George WISEHART, that had bin in the Schooles of Germany, was accused of Heresie, which he had (as was alledged against him) publiquely preached and priuately taught in Dundee, Brechin, and dyuers other parts of Scotla*n*d, since hys return home. This matter was so vrged against him, that he was conuict, and brente there in the Towne of Saint Andrewes during the time of that conuention and assembly. *Holinshed's Hist. of Scotland*, ii. 465, ed. 1577. Wishart was martyred on March 28, 1546, new style.

*th*e Realme, co*n*traire to *th*e statutis *th*airof, for *th*e particular weill of few, & hurt of mony ; the Importing of greit quantiteis of fals cun3e, sklenderlie serchit, and lychtliar punischit : The multitude of Kirkis destitute of Ministeris throw the haill cu*n*trie : The slaw administratioun of Justice, and fer les executioun : with all kynde of impieteis (as it wer) publictlie and frelie Regna*n*d.

I come now to the point that made me take up these 'Minor Poems,' notwithstanding a vow to edit no more texts for the Society for a year, and thus get a rest for my right eye weakened by long night-work. The Poems, when thrown-up by the Editor of the *Office*, came to me as the Society's servant-of-all-work. My wife had kindly copied one volume of them in a hurry years ago, when they were to have gone through the press at once. Turning past her work to Mr Brock's copy of the *Godlie Tractate*, I was so struck with the likeness of its complaints to many of those in the "Ballads and Poems on the Condition of England in Henry VIII's and Edward VI's reigns (A.D. 1520-47)," that I edited in 1868 for The Ballad Society, with a long set of illustrative extracts, that I resolved to take up the present little volume too.

Where we have in Lauder's *Godlie Tractate*, p. 20, l. 543-5,

> 3our housis halding is down, & laid on syde :
> Quhair hunders wount 3our faders to conuoye,
> Now will 3e ryde *with ane man and ane boye.*

we find in the English *Now-a-Dayes* (? ab. 1520 A.D.), l. 97-8 (Ballads from Manuscripts, p. 95),

> Tempora*ll* lordes be almost gone,
> Howsholdes kepe thei few or none,

and in Wm Stafford's Examination, 1584 A.D. (*ib.* p. 30-1), we hear the Knight complaining, though from poverty:

"so many of vs (as yee know) that haue departed out of the countrey of late, haue bene driuen to giue ouer our houshoulds, and to keepe either a chamber in London, or to wayte on the Court vncalled, *with a man and a Lackey*[1] after him, where he was wonte to

---

[1] See too the richly-clad Nobleman 'attended *with onely one Man and a Page*' contrasted with him in his former condition, 'very homely apparreled,' but with 'a hundred or sixe score proper and personable men ' after him, in *A Health to the Gentlemanly Profession of Seruing Men*, 1598, p. 155, ed. 1868, Roxburghe Library.

keepe halfe a score of cleane men in his house, and xx. or xxiii. other persons besides, euery day in the weeke."

If we have in Lauder, *Godlie Tractate*, p. 22, l. 632-5,

> For Gods wourd wes neuer moir trewlie teachit
> Nor it is now in mony placis preachit,
> And neuer sa mony vngodlie pepill sene
> In to this earth, sen it Inhabit bene !

we find in *Vox Populi*, § 8, p. 138, l. 528-534,

> Goddes worde is well sett forth ;
> hitt never was more preched,
> ner never so pleynely techede ;
> hitt never was soe halloed,
> nor never soe lyttell fowloed,
> both of hygh and lowe [*orig.* hyght and lawe].

If we find in Lauder, *Godlie Tractate*, p. 21-2, l. 600-3,

> The Mes, that Idoll—praysit be God !—is past ;
> Bot Couatyce, the quhilk is cum in last,
> Is the worst Idoll of the twa, be fer.

we see in *Vox Populi*, p. 139, l. 536-41,

> we haue banyschyd superstysyon,
> but styll we kepe ambysyon ;
> we haue showtt awaye all cloystre[r]es,
> but styll we kepe extorsyonares ;
> we haue taken there landes for ther abbwese [abuse],
> but we haue convertyd theme to a worse vse.

Indeed, my English Ballad-volume may serve as an illustrative one to the present text[1], though two bitter complaints of the people of

---

[1] The clearance I alluded to in writing was this : "In Ross-shire, accordingly, it was undertaken on a great scale in 1792. The dissatisfaction produced was so great, that the most serious affrays took place, and the military had to act, and blood was shed before quiet was restored." This is from the *couleur-de-rose* Mr James Loch, the carrier-out of the Stafford-estate clearances, in his *Account of the Improvements on the Estates of the Marquess of Stafford*, 1820, p. xviii. He says, however, that the same system of clearing men out for sheep had been carried on in the border counties 'during the period which elapsed between the union of the crowns and that of the kingdoms' of England and Scotland (*ib.* p. xvi.).

Those who wish to see how Mr Loch's *clearing* of the Stafford part of Sutherland was carried out—and sites for the Free Church refused there too—should read Hugh Miller's '*Sutherland as it was and is ; or how a Country may be ruined*': Edinburgh, 1843. On p. 4 he quotes Sismondi's parallel of

England, against the wholesale turning of arable land into pasture,—the ejectment of men for sheep—and the enclosure of commons, are not heard in Lauder's poems. For the former of these, Scotland's turn came, over two hundred years later[1], and bitter then too was the cry of her dispossessed poor. During landlords' rule, the rights of property got a good deal more enforced than its duties. The general opinion now about the Irish land-question seems to promise well for the treatment of the future English and Scotch ones.

The notes of the Editor of *The Office* were so many, on minute points of metre, inflexion, &c., that, though I disagree with several of them, I have not thought it worth while to trouble the reader with arguments about them, or to add notes on like points in the present text. Two misinterpreted words that I chance to have noticed, may be mentioned: 1. *Hearis*—p. 18, l. 520; p. 32, note on l. 520—is clearly *heirs*. 'Heirs & successors' is the regular legal and customary phrase; and as Lauder is speaking to kings, he would hardly say to them, 'you, your *Lords* and your Successors.' The Lords of Kings could only be the so-called Three Persons of the Trinity, and Lauder certainly can't have meant them. 2. *Lambmes*, Office, p. x., is not 'Lady-Mass,' but the A.Sax. '*Hláf-mæsse*, the loaf-mass or feast, Lammas-day' (Bosworth), Aug. 1, the feast of first-fruits. (This is altered in the revised edition, 1869.) As too I was originally answerable for the explanation on p. 30 of *The Office* note on the 1st *n* of *pringnant*, and the Palsgrave extract on p. 31, I may as well say that two men who know much more about the matter than I, hold me wrong. Mr J. A. H. Murray says that in Middle Scotch

---

[1] Switzerland: "If the Counts of Kyburgh, of Lentzburgh, of Hapsburgh, and of Gruyeres, had been protected by the English laws, they would find themselves at the present day precisely in the condition in which the Earls of Sutherland were 20 years ago. Some of them would perhaps have had the same taste for *improvements*, and several republics would have been expelled from the Alps, to make room for flocks of sheep."

A Defence of the Highland clearances may be seen in " Observations on the Present State of the Highlands of Scotland, with a view of the Causes and probable Consequences of Emigration," by the Earl of Selkirk, London, 1805.

To Professor Blackie's kindness I owe the references to the authorities in this note.

2. Cornelius de Vois, a Dutchman, in 1567-82, found Scotland and England 'both oppressed with poor people which beg from door to door for want of employment, and no man looketh to it.' Chambers's *Dom. Ann.* i. 50.

change of the English *gn* into *ng* and *ngn* was very common, *conding, maling, syngis* and *syngnis* (for *signs*), &c. &c. being found; and Mr Alexander J. Ellis, one of our first living authorities on Pronunciation, writes:

"I have looked to the passage in Lauder, and the note. The passage from Palsgrave (cited in note on p. 30, l. 385) has, I think, no connection with the spelling *prengnant*. The point to be considered is whether in the sixteenth century *pregnant* was taken from the French with the French pronunciation, or from Latin with the current English pronunciation of Latin. I take the latter view. Now Salesbury's spelling of the Latin words *magnus, agnus, ignis,* &c., as *mangnus, angnus, ingnis,* &c., is quite distinct. If he had heard *man-gnus*, with *gn* as in Italian, he would have written *man-niws*, I believe. In Swedish, *gn* is pronounced *ng-n*, thus *Tegnér* is called *Teng-nér*. I have learned this vivâ voce, as well as from books. Rapp (Phys. der Sprache, vol. 3, p. 241) says: 'Der Scandinavier kennt kein ng-g mehr, weder in- noch auslautend ... Folglich wird ng regelmässig durch ng, in nk durch n, *und in lateinischen Formen mit gn wie bei uns nach der Schul-Tradition durch g bezeichnet.* (Abkürzungen wie *mang* für *magnus* in der Volkssprache.) Dieses gn ist aber im Schwedischen in die wirkliche Sprache eingetreten, indem die häufige Verbindung gn durchaus in ng-n assimilirt wurde.'"

I have added sidenotes to the present Text because I found the want of them in the *Office*, to give me an Abstract of it.[1] They will at least help readers to skip those parts of the *Tractate* that look dull. One can't expect many people to read the Sermon all through. The following is a skeleton of it. The text is John xv. 6-8, from the Allegory of the Vine.

I. of those who abide not in Christ, and their burning.
II. of those who abide in Him, and their reward; and their duty to bear much fruit:—
I. 1. *a*. The non-abiders generally. *β*. specially (p. 5-6), the Romish Church, temporizers, shrinkers, flatterers, &c.
I. 2. The Torments of the Wicked (p. 6-8), and how the pains of Hell begin here by men's consciences plaguing them.

[1] This is the use of sidenotes in late Texts like the present one. The only awkwardness in reading it that I found, was, to recollect that *thir* meant 'these' and not 'their'.

II. The Godly and their Reward. 1. The Abiders in Christ described (p. 10-11).

II. 2. A. Their first Benefit. α. Oneness with Christ; and herein of the Romish Mass, and Papist Prelates' pride (p. 12-13).

β. Christ cannot be separated from his Elect (p. 14-15).

II. 2. B. Their second Benefit: they shall bring forth much fruit. Herein, Hypocrites and Covetous Protestants, the Swine, are denounced (p. 16-23), for their cruelty to the Poor in the Dearth (p. 16-17), their Harlotry (p. 19), their Extortions (p. 19-20), their Pride and Avarice (p. 20-23).

II. 2. C. The third Benefit of the Abiders: they shall be true disciples. And herein of the Scotch Martyrs (p. 24).

The other Minor Poems are sufficiently explained by their titles. The illustrative extracts about the subjects of these Poems might have easily been carried to much greater length, and with some justification, as most of us down South are no doubt profoundly ignorant of the state of Scotland in the 16th century—I know I am;—but as Lyndesay's Works [1] and *The Complaynt of Scotland*, ab. 1548, both deal so largely with the subject, and are both soon to be completed for the Society, I have been content to let the foregoing extracts and references suffice for the present occasion. The one poet from whose works above all I should have quoted most largely, Sir Richard Maitland of Lethingtoun, Knicht, Lauder's contemporary, and who wrote on the same themes as he, I have, after some hesitation, resolved not to quote here at all, because I should want so much of him that I prefer to edit his poems for the Society, or to get them so edited, as a little companion volume to the present one. Meantime, if any reader cares to follow up the subject, let him read in Pinkerton's "Ancient Scottish Poems [2] never before in Print," 1786, vol. ii. p. 298—345, Maitland's "Satire on the Age"; "*On the Miseries of the Tyme*, 1570"; "The World worth na Thocht"; "Public Miserie the Frute of Vice"; "Aganis Oppressioun of the Com-

[1] The *Satyre* is a wonderfully living picture of the time, 1535-9 A.D. See our *Report* for Jan. 1869, p. 12-13.

[2] Or in the Maitland Club edition of Sir R. Maitland's Poems, &c., ed Jos. Bain, 1830, from the Drummond MS., Edinburgh, with Moral and Religious Poems left out by Pinkerton.

mouns"; "Na Kyndnes at Court without Siller"; "Satire on the Toun Ladyes"; "Complaint against the lang Law-sutes"; "On the World's Ingratitude"; and "To King James VI."

The Rev. Walter Gregor, of Pitsligo Manse—the writer of the able essay on the Banffshire Dialect and the Glossary of Words not in Jamieson's Dictionary, in the Philological Society's *Transactions*, 1866—has been kind enough to fill-in those parts of the Biblical and other references in the *Godlie Tractate* which the binder, after the cursed custom of his craft,[1] had pared off, and to add the verses in justification of his insertions.

My thanks are due, 1. to Mr S. Christie-Miller of Britwell House, Burnham, Bucks, for letting me collate the proofs and revises of this Text with his unique originals, which he kindly brought to London for the purpose: 2. to Mr David Laing, for his Additional Note at the head of this Preface; for the loan of his woodcut of the Mirror from which the casts for our titles have been taken; also for the loan of his copy of *The Office* from which our facsimile of its title[2] has been admirably drawn and cut on wood by Mr W. H. Hooper of my corps; lastly, for his kind offices with Mr Christie-Miller; 3. to Mr James A. H. Murray for notes and hints.

 3, *St George's Square, Primrose Hill, London, N.W.*
  18 *January*, 1870.

[1] The copy of Scott's first edition of Lyndesay's *Monarché*, that formerly belonged to Dr Leckie, has been served in the same way, seemingly by an Edinburgh binder, who, or whose men, have considered that Sir David's name was Sir *Duod*—their reading of 'Quod' Lyndesay, in the Colophon, that G is E, and therefore sheet G should go before sheet E, and that F ii comes before F i, which should follow F 4!

[2] This should be bound in the *Office*, after its modern title-page.

P.S. I see the name *Lawder* in vol. ii. of Knox's Works. In May, 1562, the Swedish Ambassador, Herr Peter Groif, 'logeit in Mr Harie LAWDER's lodgeing' (*Diurnal of Occurrents*, p. 72-3), quoted in Laing's *Knox's Works*, ii. 335, note [4]; and Mr Laing thinks that in the same lodging the General Assembly met on 29 June, 1562, *ib.* p. 337, note[1]; but he holds that neither this Harie nor any other of the many Lauders known, are of the poet's family.

Mr James A. H. Murray, having only just had the Society's 1864 edition of Lauder's *Office* brought under his notice, sends me a long list of corrections for it, of which those on the next page are the most important. To such of them as have been already made in the 2nd edition, I have prefixed a †.

CORRECTIONS FOR LAUDER'S *OFFICE*,

E. E. TEXT SOC., 1864.

p. 3, l. 14. *dede*, of course 'death,' not 'deed.'

p. 3, l. 23. *bye*, of course 'buy (off),' not 'avail, stand in stead.'

p. 5, l. 63. *Nothing at all* is the ordinary English phrase.

p. 5, l. 69, and note on it, p. 25-6. Read 'sched also—quha vnderstude—.' *Also* has its ordinary meaning here. The mistake of thinking it means *as* in Scotch, like it does in Early English, vitiates the whole of the Notes, &c. *Quha* is 'whosoever.'

† p. 5, l. 80. *to-spent*, no infinitive, but a participle, with the common intensive prefix *to*.

p. 6, l. 103. *for pure pakkis*, 'elucidated' as 'merely because of agreements.' The phrase 'puir packs' I have often heard in common talk in Scotland : it's the English 'sorry pelf.' The reference is of course, as Chalmers points out, to the *pack* of the pedlar or travelling merchant (an important personage still in rural districts, much more so in past times when intercommunication was difficult). From the *pack* containing the merchants' whole worth, wealth, or stock in trade, the word was transferred so as to mean 'estate, gear, wealth, riches, money.' A fraudulent bankrupt who "feathers his nest," is said in Scotland to "make up his *pack;*" when a spendthrift is going through the paternal estate, people shake their head and say " He 'll soon be at the boddum o' the *pack!*"

p. 6, l. 114, and note on it, p. 28. *That* is the demonstrative adjective : '*That* Kyng,' namely God. 'The is [*not*] here to be supplied.'

p. 9, l. 193. *Also* means 'also' and not 'as.' Lines 193-4 therefore read— 'unless their lieges also, be godly men, perfectly knowing (doing know) God's word.'

† p. 9, l. 207. *on hycht* (Gloss. p. 35, col. 2), on high, aloud ; *altè clamans*.

† p. 10, l. 224. *paird*, not 'impaired,' but 'pared, cut down.'

† p. 10, l. 226. *trewtwiche stone*, true touchstone.

† p. 10, l. 236. *syne* is the A.S. *siððan*, sithence, since ; not *sæne*, slow.

p. 11, l. 260. *pose* is hoard.

† p. 11, l. 282. *gude* is 'goods,' possessions (Fr. *bien*), not 'rank.'

p. 16, l. 428. *ledgin*, 'alledging,' citing, not 'book, learning.'

p. 16, l. 442. *leid*, 'lead,' not 'let, permit' ; cp. to '*lead* evidence,' '*ducere carmen*,' &c.

p. 17, l. 466. *buddis*, offers (a *bid* at an auction).

p. 23. The theory expressed in the notes, p. 23, as to a dissyllabic pronunciation of *pe-ace, bo-ith, gud-e, tham-e, Godds*, seems very funny to a Scotchman ; the lines in question merely want the first short syllable, a liberty taken by all poets from Chaucer to Burns.

— Wo / be to / thame that / dois knaw
Godds wourd / syne dois / the con / trar schaw.

p. 35, col. 1. *Governall* is not 'governance,' but the Fr. *gouernail*, helm, rudder ; steering.

Ane Godlie Tractate

Or Mirrour. Quhairintill may be easilie perceauit quho Thay be that ar Ingraftit in to Christ, and quho ar nocht. Declaring also the rewaird of the Godlie and Punyschement of the Wekit. Maid bpone this pairt of Text. Writtin in the Fyftene Chaptour of the Euangell of Jhone. As followis. [*]

[*] **G**Eue ane man byde nocht in me, he is cassin furth, as ane Branche that widderis. And men gadderis thame, and castis thame in the fyre, and thay burne. Geue ȝe abyde in me & my wourdis also in to ȝow. Ask quhat ȝe wil, it salbe done bnto ȝow. Wirin is my Father Glorefyit, that ȝe bryng furth mekle frute, and be maid my [†]

[†] Disceplis. ¶ Compylд In Meter, be William Lauder, Minister of the Wourd of God. For yᵉ Instructioun comfort and consolatioun of all Faithfull Christianes. To quhome he wissith, Grace, Mercie, and Peace, in Jesus Christ our Lord and onlie Sauiour. So be it.

L Uke in this Mirrour, and thow sall cleirlie se,
Gyf yᵘ be Reprobat, or chosin, it sal declair to the.

3

¶ The Content*is* of this Buke. [A i. back]

☞ TO THE REDAR.

Ll faithfull, herkin, & to my word*is* attend, — Faithful folk,
And ernistlie do merk thame til ane end;
Ponder thame weill, a*nd* wey thaim in ȝour hart; — weigh well my words!
Ilk stait of ma*n*, *co*nsider ȝour awi*n* part, 4
And Iudge me nocht, that I haue done indyte — I have written this Tractate
This lytle Tractate of malice or dispyte,
Bot for ane warnyng to the impenitent, — to warn the impenitent, and
And for the confort of thame that doth repent, 8 — comfort the penitent.
As may all faithfull graip, and als considder,
Layand the Text and this my werk togidder,
¶ Humblie exhorting euerie Creature,
Learnd, vnlearnd, auld, ȝung, ryche and pure, 12
To take heirfor my sayings in gude part, — Take my sayings, therefore, in good part!
Sen I do write thame of ane zealus hart,
As God me Iudge, quho knawis *th*e mynd & thocht
Of euerye wicht that in this warld is wrocht. 16
So to my Text now breuelie to proceid,
Grit God me help, and with his spreit me speid!

¶ THE DIUISIOUN OF THE TEXT.

My text is John xv. 6—8.

This part of Text[1] quhilk I am to discyde,
In to two head*is*—will God—I sall deuyde: 20 — I divide it into 2 heads:
¶ The first head, the punyscheme*nt* sall be — I. 1. the punishment of sinners,
Of wekit Synnair*is* for thair Iniquytie;

---

[1] As the Text (from the allegory of the Vine) is standing on its head at the left of the Mirror in the Title page, it is re-

2. the torments of the despisers of God's word.	And speciallie, the torment*is* heir I schaw	
	Of thame that dois contem God*is* wourd & Law,	24
	And how the wekit ar nocht ingraft in Christ,	
	Bot ar the Children of the Antechrist.	
II. the rich reward of the Godly. [sign. A ii.]	¶ The secund head sall be the riche rewaird	
	The Godlie gett*is*, quhilk dois thair God regaird,	28
	And how tha ar ingraft in Christ Iesu,	
Iho. x[v.]	Be the imbracing of his wourd most trew.	

¶ THE DISCRIPTIOUN OF THE FIRST HEAD.

I. 1. then, of the	SO now returnand till our first head agane,	
	Aduert, and ȝe sall heir the crewell pane,	32
terrible decree	The sorrowfull Sentence and terribill decreit,	
	In to few wourd*is* ar heir contenit compleit,	
against the wicked and vicious.	That is prepaird for wekit Creaturs,	
	And vicius men that in to Uice indurs.	36
	¶ For thame that drownd ar in Idolatrie,	
	For poysond pepill with Infidelytie,	
	For stif contemnars of gods lyuelie wourd,	
	This suthfast Sentence; allace, it is no bourd!	40
Math. [v.]	It is no Sentence be Man retreattabill,	
i. Peter [iv.]	It is no Sentence be man debaittabill,	
Esa. lvi[ii.] It is a judgment that no man can revoke, that spares neither king nor poor.	It nowthair sparis King nor Empriour,	
	Duke, Erll, Lord, nor pussant Conquyrour;	44
	It nowthair sparis mychtie men nor pure,	
Iere. i.	That of the wourd of God doith tak no cure;	
	Bot is ane Sentence quhilk none can do eschew	
	That dois contem the wourd of Christ Iesu.	48
I. 1. I take the folk who abide not in Christ.	This Sentence merkit, the pepill we discus	
	That doith nocht abyde in Christ Iesus.	

printed here from the ordinary modernization of the Autho‧ized Version:

6 "If a man abide not in me, he is cast forth as a branc[h] and is withered; and men gather them, and cast *them* in[to]
7 the fire, and they are burned. If ye abide in me, and m[y] words abide in you, ye shall ask what ye will, and it sha[ll]
8 be done unto you. Herein is my Father glorified, that y[e] bear much fruit; so shall ye be my disciples."

ANE GODLIE TRACTATE OR MIRROUR.

¶ ANE GENERALL DISCRIPTIOUN OF THAME
THAT BYDIS NOCHT IN CHRIST.

A. *generally.*

IN Christ tha byde nocht, we do vnderstand,
The quhilk, aggreing vnto his command,
Dois nocht imbrace his wourd most louynglie,
With feruent mynd and hart most constantlie,
And in that wourd hes nocht ane solyde faith :
Thir bydis nocht in Christ, the Scripture saith,
Bot ar Inuoluit in-to dung-hill*is* of Sin,
And euerye daye frome Sin to Sin tha rin.

52

56

Those who obey not His command, embrace not His word,

and have not firm faith in it.

[A. ii. back]

¶ It sufficis nocht that we Baptizit be,
Bot it requyris als, of necessitie,
That we contynew in Christs Euangell trew,
Or ell*is* we can nocht byde in Christ Iesu.

60

Baptism alone is no good.
[I]hon. xv.
Math. x.
[ii.] Tim. ii.
We must continue in Christ's Gospel.

¶ ANE DISCRIPTIOUN OF THAME IN SPECIALL
THAT BYDIS NOCHT IN TO CHRIST.

I. 1. *B. specially.*
These abide not in Christ:

THe Romane Kirk, and all of that degre,
Quhilk dois menteane peruerst Idolatrie,
Sic as the Messe, (quhilk is plane derogatioun
To Christ[i]s glore and his most blissed Passioun,)
With all the rabill of tha Sophist*is* and Clerks
That doith ascryue Saluatioun to thair werks,
Or attribut*is* Remissioun of thair Sin
To ony wicht that is the warld within,
Tha pepill, I say, doith nocht abyde in Christ,
Bot ar the Children of the Antechrist.

64

68

72

α. the Roman Church, those who
[G]al. ii. a*nd*
[iii.]
uphold Idolatry like the Mass.

β. those who ascribe salvation to works, or remission of sins to any mortal.

¶ Thir Temporesars doith nocht in Christ abyde,
Neathir thir schrinkars that fro*m* t*h*e treuth dois slyde,
Neathir thir flattrers, that for feir of thair bags
Dois wag about aye as the busse it wags,
Neathir tha pepill that for feir of thair lyues,
And tinsall of thair houshald*is*, bairnis, and wyues,
And lose of guds, [&] gear, or wardlie rent,
Frome God[i]s wourd thame selues doith absent ;

76

80

γ. temporisers,
δ. shrinkers,
[I]say. iii.
[I]aco. i.
ε. flatterers,

[L]uc. ix.
[a]nd xiiii.
Math. x.
ζ. stayers-away from God's word for fear of losing life or goods.

	ANE GODLIE TRACTATE OR MIRROUR.

<small>η. or for their Prince's pleasure; [A]ct. iiii.</small> Nor tha that dois, for pleasure of thair Prence,
Refuse Gods wourd, of maist magnificence.

<small>θ. folk divided, not giving both soul and body to God;</small> ¶ And sure it is, quho treulie list discydit,[1]
God will nocht haue that man that is deuydit ;   84
Bot he will haue him, Saule and bodye haill ;

<small>[ii.] Cor. vi.</small> Quho is deuydit, his faith doith nocht auaill.

<small>ι. dissemblers.</small> Dissemblit pepill doith nocht abyde in Christ,
Bot ar the children of the Antechrist.   88

<small>[A 2 ; no sig.]</small> ¶ And as the faithfull in Christ ingraftit be,
Be his Euangell and wourd of Ueritie,

<small>Iho. viii. and xv. These are the Church Malignant, grafted into Satan.</small> So is the Kirk malignant, but more plead,
Ingraft in Sathan,—of that ilk kirk thair head,—   92
With dewillysche doctrine, and Idolatrie
Of thame that speyk*is* leis throw Ypocresie.

<small>I. 2. *The torments of the Wicked.*</small>   ¶ OF THE GREUOUS TORMENTIS
      PREORDINAT FOR THE WEKIT.

Quhat end mak*is* thir to proceid furthirmair ?

<small>Ioan. xv. They are cast out like a dry, lopt branch,</small> Tha ar cast furth, *the* Text this doith declair, 93
Maist lyke ane branche doun cuttit of ane stok,
That is becum ane drye and widderit blok.
Meit for no werk that man wald do desyre,

<small>to be thrown in the fire.</small> Bot to be brint, and cassin in ane fyre.   100
Euin so the curst Contemnar*is* of the treuth,

<small>Wicked doers</small> And wekit wirkars, for thair Sin and sleuth,

<small>Gal. v.</small> That will nocht do the wourd of Christ imbrace,

<small>are dry of grace;</small> Ar clene dryit vp frome euerye kynd of grace,   104
And hes no pairt with Christ, nor with his glore,
Moir nor the widderit branche, the quhilk before
I said had Iusse or Sapour of the tre,
Quhen it is cuttit, and dois frome growing de.   108

<small>dry with the heat of lust, having no juice of the Spirit,</small> ¶ Tha ar cum drye with Lust and carnall heit,
Because tha want the Sapour of the spreit
Of Christ Iesus, the Sauiour of man.
Wanting this Iusse, quhairfor ar tha meit than ?   112

<small>[1] discyde it.</small>

or nothing ellis,—the text it schewis plane,—
Bot to sustene of Hellis fyre the pane,
As Nero sufferit for his tirrannye,
And Pharao for his grit Ydolatrie, 116
And as the gluttoun quho refusit Lazarus,
With mony mo nor heir I may discus.

¶ So thus the wekit; tha get no vther hyre, [A 2, back]
Bot for thair Sin ar brint in flam of fyre, 120
Ay daylie deand, and neuer ʒit can de ;
Thus end*is* the wekit, for thair Iniquytie.

¶ Bot lat ws heir the text perfytlie feill,
And lat ws merk the wourd*is* thairof richt weill, 124
As quhair it sayis nocht that, 'that man sall be
'Cast furth that bydis nocht in Christ constantlie,'
Bot speykand in the present tyme it sayis,
"He is reieckit now instantlie alwayis." 128
Albeit on lyfe that ʒit he leuand be,
He is cast furth : the text this latts ws se.
So heir the text pronuncis till ws plat,
That Christ, he speykis heir of the reprobat ;—[1] 132
For as the faithfull, now leuyng heir but more,
Ar partakers with Christ in heauinnis glore,
And dois begin thair heauin in earth heir doun,
Quhen as tha thole soir persecutioun 136
For richtyusnes, takand in pacience
All earthlie trubill, knawand thair Innocence,
Hayfand respect, and still in memore,
The heauinnis Ioye and grit felicite 140
That thay at last be Christ ar till obtene,
Quhen as tha knaw thair conscience is clene
Of sik Iniury as wes thair accusatioun,
This earthlie trubill is thair grit consolatioun, 144
Quhilk consolatioun, it is the waye full euin,
And pleasand passage, vnto the port of heauin.

Ioan. xv.
Exo. iiii. [v.]
vi. vii. vi[ii.]
fit only
for Hell-fire,
like Nero,
Pharaoh, and
Luc. ix.
Dives.

Ihon. xv.
So end the
wicked ;
daily dying,
never dead !
Math. iii.
Esa. lxvi.

But mark, the
text says not
shall be cast
forth,

Ihon. iii.
and xv.
but *is* cast forth,
though alive,

if he be reprobate.
For, as the
Faithful
[I]hon. v.
begin their
heaven on earth,

[i] Pet. iiii.
taking patiently
all earthly
trouble,

as their road to
the gate of
Heaven,

[1] The following parenthesis comprises 28 lines, lasting to
l. 160.

The quhilk begynnis in to this wrachit ground,

according to what the Scripture says, As in the Scripture cleirlie may be found, 148
Quhair as it sayis, and writtin is expres,
"Be mony trublis, sorrowis, and distres,

Act. iiii. "[1] The godlie sall in heauin haue thair Intrance,
[1 A 1; no sig.] Thair to posses thair Iust inheritance." 152
¶ Euin so all thay, to speyk in wourd*is* breue,
That godlie will in to Christ Iesus leue,

ii Tim. iii. Man thame addres, his Croce for to vptake,
And suffer persecutioun for his saike, 156

and what the example of Heb. ii. ¶ As the Appostil*is* and Propheits nocht possest
The heauinnis glore in earth with wardlie rest,
Apostles and Prophets teaches, Bot sum tholit death, and sum richt sore torment,
Heir vpon earth, or tha till heauin vp went;— 160
¶ Directlie speakand in the contrarie,

even so the wicked, who know the word of God and work against it, Of wekit pepill that leuis sinfullie,
To quhome also is knawin the woud of God,
And wilfullie dois rin the contrair rod 164
In werk and wourd, in thocht and in Intent
Expresse aganis the Lordis commandiment,

Heb. vi. and x. have no peace in their conscience; and so begin here the pains of Hell. Contynewand thus in thair Sin and offence,
This man can neuer haue peace in conscience; 168
Quhilk peace quho want*is*, *the* treuth most trew to tel,
Is the begynning of the paynis of Hell.

Quhilk paynis infernal begynnis lykewyse, we se,
In this vale of misery, In to this earth, and Uaill of miserie. 172
Quho wants this rest and peace of conscience,
Of this may haue ane sure experience.

their conscience barks at them; For quhill he leuis, his conscience tryis[2] and berks
[2 ? *for* cryis.] Gods wraith to wrak him for his wekit werks; 176
and after death accuses them. Quhen he is dead, his conscience sall accuse him,
And him condamp, quhair he hes done abuse him.

And as the living Faithful have each his appointed place in Heaven, ¶ And as the faithfull, now leuand heir on lyfe,
Of all degre, baith Infant, man, and wyfe, 180
Hes now in Heauin, of Gods especiall grace,
Ilk ane thair awin preparit roum and place,

¶ So hes the wekit leuand, I ȝow tell,	[A 1, back]	so have the living wicked, in Hell.
Ik ane thair awin appoyntit rowmes in Hell.	184	
¶ To tell quho ar Eleckit or refusit,		Who are elect, who rejected,
can nocht saye ; thairin hald me excusit ;		
In nane thair-of haue sik experience		each must ask himself.
As man him self, grapand his awin conscience.	188	
¶ Lyke as the man that finds his lyfe aggre		He is elect who lives by God's word,
To Gods command and wourd of verite,		
And hes ane feruent mynd to perseueir		
Under the reull of God[i]s wourd sinceir,	192	
Syne dois continew as Gods word dois direc him,		and continues in it.
That man may knaw that God hes done elec him ;		
And with the wekit, thocht still he be suspeckit,		
ȝit still the faithfull may compt him as eleckit.	196	
¶ And in the contrair, accompt this for no bourd,		He is rejected who contemns God's word,
Quho dois contempne of God the lyuelie wourd,		
And dois menteine peruerst Idolatrie,		upholds idolatry,
And will nocht cum to heir the veritie,	200	
And quha that cummis to heir, and dois abuse it,		
And quha hes hard, syne efter dois refuse it,		or refuses the Truth, turning, like a dog, to his vomit.
Turnand as Tykis vnto thair vomatyue,—		
As sum hes done, that leuand ar on lyue,—	204	
¶ Contynewand this[1] in to thair odius Sin,		
Ending thair lyuis as than tha do begin ;		
I can nocht say, nor on na wayis excuse thame,		Luc. xii.
Bot force man grant that God hes done refuse thame.	208	

¶ THE EXHORTATIOUN VPON THE FIRST HEAD.

I. concluded.

Quhairfor I do Imploir with humbill hart		I pray you, then, consider,
Ilk man in earth, to ponder thair awin part,		
And to considder in to quhat stait tha stand,		Are you with God, or against Him ?
Quhidder with God, or contrair his command,	212	
[2] That he that stands may stand, and nocht do fall,		i. Cor. x.
And quho hes fallin, may knaw the sam at all[3] ;		Have you fallen ?

[1] this = thus : see p. 29, l. 85.
[2] sign. B.   [3] ? thoroughly, or at all events.

Then pray to God for grace to rise again,	Syne praye to God in to most hartlie wyse,	
	To grant thame grace vp frome thair fall to ryse,	216
	And to contynew in Christ*is* Euangell trew,	
and be grafted into Christ.	And so Ingraftit in to Christ Iesu.	
	This fer, deir brether, sall stand for the first heid;	
	Nixt to the Secund, schortlie I proceid.	220

II. *The Reward of the Godly.* (*With the Devillish Doctrine of the Papists*, p. 12—15; *and the Hellish Selfishness and Covetousness of the so-called Protestants*, p. 16—23.)

¶ HEIR ENDIS THE FIRST HEAD. AND FOLLOWIS THE SECUND HEAD. WITH THE TEXT THAIROF.

Gᴇᴜᴇ ȝe abyde in me, and my wourdis also
In to ȝow, Ask quhat ȝe will, It sal be done vnto ȝow. Heirin is my Father Glorefyit, That ȝe
bring furth mekill Fructe, and be maid my
Disciplis. Iohan. xv.

&c.

Of the profit of the unity between Christ and his Church	THe Fructe, the proffeit, and the commodytie In to this gratius and Godlie Unitie	
	Betuix Christ Iesus and his Kirk most trew,	
He speaks here, to comfort His disciples,	Lo, Christ he dois heir furthirmore ensew.	224
	To mak the consolatioun the moir	
	Of his Discyplis, he speak*is* the sam heirfoir;	
	And for to draw thame till ane constancie,	
and show them that if they abide in Him,	He schewis thame the grit Utilitie	228
	That followis thame that in him dois abyde,	
	In to few wourds he dois the sam discyde:	
	Christ sayis thir wourds, "gyf ȝe will byde in me,	
they get 3 great benefits. Ioan. xv.	" Thairthrow ȝe sall obtene grit proffitt*is* thre."	232
	¶ Bot quhat ar tha that dois in Christ remane?	
II. 1. Those that abide in Christ i Ioan. i[i] are those who embrace His [sign. B back] [I]oan. viii. word and are engrafted into Him by faith.	Tha kynd of pepill the Text declaris plane:	
	"Euin tha," it sayis, "that dois my wourd*is* imbrace,	
	" Tha same in me, tha haue ane dwelling place,	236
	" And tha be faith in me ar still Ingrauit,	
	" And I in thame thairthrow rychtso consauit."	
	So this Coniunctioun and this Unitie	
	Betuix Christ Iesus and his Kirk trewlie,	240

[ȝ be no meanis bot be his wourd imbrasing,
And it in to thair Inwert Bowell*is* placing,
ιs wes of Abraham, and mony faithfull mo :
ᴛo cearche the Scripture, and thow sall find it so. 244

¶ We find nocht heir the Paip, that Antechrist,
Doith ws Conione vnto our Maister Christ ;
ᴠor we perceaue nocht heir that our ingrauyng
ᴵs in to Christ be our Byschopis receauyng, 248
ᴀs be Annoynting, and schauing of our Croun ;
ᵂe find nocht heir sic vaine Coniunctioun ;
ᴮot onlie find*is* ws Ingraft in Christ Iesu
Be the imbrasing of his wourd most trew. 252

¶ And quho so thus with Christ Conioynit be,
May be assurit to get thir proffitt*is* thre,
The quhilk in ordour, as tha stand in the Text,
I sall declair, Ilkane till vthir Annext. 256

[i] Ioan. ii.
That is the only means.
[R]om. iii.
[I]bid.

No Pope,
[i] Ioan. ii.

248 no Bishop's receiving, no anointing or crown-shaving!

[i] Ioan. ii.
252 [i] Iho. ii.
Only, the embracing His word.
Those thus joined to Christ get the 3 benefits in the Text.

¶ THE FIRST COMMODITE OF THAME THAT ABYDIS
IN TO CHRIST.

II. 2. *a. the first Benefit:*

¶ THE TEXT.

☞ ASK QUHAT ȜE WILL. IT SALL BE
GEUIN VNTO ȜOW.

☞ (✠) ☜
⁎

First, in this Spirituall Unioun we haue
  Quhat richtius thi*n*g of Christ *that* we sal craue.
¶ Quhat better thing can man seik for his hyre,
Nor get all thing he Iustlie will desyre? 260
No better thing can onye crayf or wys,
In to this earth on lyfe that leuing is,
Nor haue all thingis to thame performit and done
That Godlie is, be the grit God abone, 264
For the imbrasing of his wourd most trew,
And so to be Ingraft in Christ Iesu.

[I]oan. xv.
What right thing we ask, we have.

No better reward can any one conceive on earth ;
[B ii : no sig.]
Ioan. xv.
i Ioan. [ii.]

and he is daft who lacks it, since he can get it so easily.	I compt thame daft, and mekill wors nor mad, That laykis this gift, so lichtlie may be had, Sekand the sam vpon ane vther ground, Quhilk¹ be no vther maner can be found.	268
II. 2. A. a. Since, then, we are one with Christ in spirit, Ioan. vi[i.] et.xvi. it is but vanity to desire his body here. The Spirit quickens; the flesh profits nothing.	¶ Sen Christ hes promist this to his faithful all, Be this Coniunctioun and Unioun Spirituall, I saye it is bot verraye Uanytie For to desyre Christ with ws corporallie. ¶ It is the Spreit that quyknis auld and ȝing; The corporall flesche, it proffittis no thing: "Without," sayis Christ, "my body do ascend, The Confortour to ȝow I can nocht send."	272 276
Christ must needs go up to His Father Mar. vi[ii.] Luc. iiii. Ioan. xv[i.] Heb. x. Act. vii. Ioan. xv[i.] till he comes down to judge the world. Papists can't show He's descended yet. How then can they make and eat him bodily?	¶ Thus it behouit Christ of necessitie Unto the Father to passe vp reallie, Quhair he abydis, and euer sall remane Quhill he discend to Iudge the warld agane. For vthirwyse, gyf Christ had nocht ascendit, The holy Gost till ws had nocht discendit. ¶ Thow can not, Papist, be Scripture mak it kend That Christ sensyne did corporallie discend. How is it than thow thinkis no schame to le, To say thow makis him, and eytis him carnallie?	280 284 288
Why can't the Popish Church have spiritual union with Christ? Because they seek him in the Ioan. vi[i.] flesh. [Ma]th. xvi. As, while the Apostles [M]ath. xvi. [x]xv. thought Christ'd [I]oan. viii. be a temporal King,	¶ Now may it heir be sperit and demandit, And gude it wer that we suld vnderstandit,² Quhat is the cause the Kirk Papisticall Can neuer haue this Unioun Spirituall Of Christ Iesus trewlie in thame ingrauit? The cause is this, sa fer as I perceauit,³ That so lang as tha seyk him carnallie, Tha can no wayis posses him Spirituallie. [B ii, back] As the Appostillis, beleuing Christ to ring In earth amangs thame as ane temporall King, So lang as tha of this had Esperance, Tha euer leuit still in Ignorance,	292 296 300

¹ Quhllk *in orig.*   ² understand it.   ³ perceive it.

And neuer knew quhat Christ ment in his teaching, [Lu]c. ix.
For all his daylie and contynewall preaching ; they never knew what His teaching meant,
No moir sall neuer no carnall Creature— so no carnal
So lang as tha sall fleschelie Folk*is* Indure,— 304 creature can know God's word
Cum to the knowledge and intelligence [i C]or. ii.
Of God[i]s wourd, and Spirituall pure sentence,
Thocht Angell*is* wer to preache it to thame plane ; though angels
Preue quho so please, thair laubour sall be vane. 308 preach it to him.

¶ Now falls it weill to vs to wey but moir, Why too did
Quhat wes the cause, the reasoun, and quhairfoir [Hug]o Be-[ren]g. de
The Papistis said 'tha maid Christ Reallie [Tour]se.
' In to thair Messe, and Eate him carnallie.' 312 [Colo]s. ii.
                                                     the Papists say
¶ As I perceaue, it wes, that tha and thairs they make and eat Christ bodily?
Mycht stylit be "most holy God-makairs," Because they wanted to be
And thairthrow cum to warldlie Pomp and gloir, styled God-makers, and get
Richt as tha did ;—for nane micht clim to moir ; 316 worldly glory.
For Papis precellit the Kings in Dignytie, And so they did get it:
And Cardinals wes Compan3eonis to our Kings ; Popes were over Kings, and
For with my Eis my self did se thir things ;— Cardinals companions to
This mouit thame that werk till Interpryse, 320 them.
Quhilk montit thame on sic ane prydfull wyse. I saw this with my own eyes.

¶ And thocht su*m* schaifling wald haue ilk nycht in And tho' a
  cure schaveling lay all night with a
Ane Co*n*cubyne, ane Harlote, or ane Hure, whore,
With gaping, Iowking, with mony bek and nod, 324 yet in the morning he'd
Upon the morne he wald haue maid 3ow God ! make God!

¶ Sa lyke, sa lyke, as it wes trew to be, Likely, indeed!
Quhen nane of thame could mak ane lytill fle ! [B 2] When he couldn't even make a flea!
And 3it no schame, to tak in hand, tha thocht, 328 And yet he'd take in hand to
To mak grit God, quhilk maid all thing of nocht ! make the great God!
Grit God we pray, sen Prencis wald perceaue, Would to God that Princes
And it in to thair hart[i]s deiplie graue, would see how
How be tha Iuglours tha haue bene blindlynes led, they've been fed with devils'
With deuillysche Doctrine fosterit and fed ! 333 doctrine by these jugglers!
Na dout, gude Lord, bot than tha wald refuse it,
Quhen as tha knew how tha haue bene abuse-it !

¶ ANE QUESTIOUN DIRECT TO ALL PAPISTIS, DEMANDING GYF CHRIST CAN BE SEPARET FROME THE FAITHFULL.

<small>II. 2. A. β.
Can Christ be separated from the faithful?
Mathew. xxviii.
No! he is ever with his Elect,
Esay. xlv.
Psal. c.xx. ix.
to keep them from great sins,</small>

Can Christ be frome thame, that he do[is] stil sup-
    port,   336
And grants to thame thair will in lauchfull sort?
No! thair is none of Iudgement discreit,
Can saye bot he is present in the Spreit
Still in to thame that ar his trew Eleckit,   340
Least tha alwayis with Sin suld be subieckit,

<small>like theft and murder.
Tho' they sin 7 times a day,</small>

  ¶ I mene, with grit and odious transgressioun,
Siclyke as thift, reif, murthour, and oppressioun;
  ¶ For thocht the richtyus doith seuin tymes daylie
    Sin,   344
ʒit dois he nocht contynew still thairin;
For, be his Spreit Christ geuis thame Iudgement

<small>they repent,</small>

To knaw thair Sin; syne maks thame to repent,
So that tha do nocht in thair Sin delyte,   348

<small>and mourn for their sins,
like David and the Magdalene.</small>

Bot murnis thairfor with conscience contryte,
As Dauid, Peter, and the Magdalene,
With mony mo nor heir I may contene.

<small>Heb. i.
Christ is with them too, as Ruler of all the Faithful.</small>

  ¶ Christ als is with thame, as Uicar generall,   352
Rewlar and gydar of the faithfull all,
Without quhais spreit no gude thing can be wrocht;
Without his help our strenth aualis nocht;

<small>Act. xvii.
In Him we live and move;</small>

In him we leue and mouis quhill we indure,   356
It is he onlie, that taks on ws cure;   [B 2, back]

<small>He is ever with us.</small>

Thus none can saye, but Christ most certanlie
Is be his Spreit with ws contynewallie.

<small>Therefore He told his Church here before He suffered,
Ioan. xiiii.</small>

So till his Kirk, Christ heir before his Passioun   360
Repeatis thir wourdis, to gyf thame consolatioun,
That tha in that suld nocht discuragit be
For his deperting frome thame corporallie,

<small>Mathew. xxviii.</small>

Bot be his Spreit he promist stil support thame;   364
So on this wayis Christ Iesus did confort thame,

" Howbeit," sayis he, " I am to passe abone;   'tho' I must go above, yet what
" Ask quhat ʒe will, it sall to ʒow be done ;   ye ask shall
" Prouyding alwayis that ʒe constant be   368   be done,
" Abyding at my wourd of Uerite."   if ye abide in Me.'

¶ This consolatioun dois serue for ws also,   This comfort is for us now too.
Assuring ws, quhair euer we ryde or go,
Ʒe, euin amyd our Inymeis most grit,   372   [R]om. xv.
He euer is with ws present in the spreit,   Even amid our [L]uc. xxi.
Preseruing ws, and doing ws defend,   Mathew.
As he hes promist, vnto the war[l]dlis end.   [xx]viii. foes, He is with

¶ Now haue ʒe herd the first commoditie,   376   us, to the world's
The riche rewaird, and grit vtilitie,   end.
Breiflie discussit, of thame that ar ingrauit
In to Christ Iesus, and how it is conceauit.
Now herkin fordwart ; and ʒe sall schortlie heir   380
The Secund proffeit, discussit in ordour cleir

¶ THE DISCRIPTIOUN OF THE SECUND COMMO-   II. 2. B.
DITIE OF THAME THAT ABYDIS IN CHRIST.   *The Second Benefit.*

¶ THE TEXT.

Heirin is my Father Glorifyit, that
Ʒe bring furth mekill fruct. &c.

THe Secund proffeit, we sal bring furth gude frute,   We shall bring forth good fruit,
And of gude werk*is* sal not be destitute,   Ioan. xv.
That dois Gods wourd into thair harts imbrace,   [B 1]   Math. v. that is, do good works.
Making it thair to haue ane dwelling place.
For as the day can nocht be without lycht,
Nor the cleir Sone withouttin beames bricht,
The flammyng fyre without Calyditie,   388   As fire *must* give out heat,
Or without water can be the raging Se,
No more the godlie (as writt*is* cunnyng Clerk*is*,)
Can gudlie¹ be withouttin godlie werk*is*,   so the godly
With quhilks tha do the Father glorefie,   392   *must* do good works.
That ringand is in to the Heauin most hie.

¹ *? for* godlie.

ANE GODLIE TRACTATE OR MIRROUR.

Iaco. ii.
The good fruit is godly deeds.
Math. iii.
as pure doctrine sincerely preacht,

¶ This frute, but dout, tha ar the godlie deids
Quhilk from Christ Iesus, the faithfull wine, proceids,
As is the Doctrine of his wourd most pure   396
Sinceirlie Preacheit to euerie Creature,

which converts men from vice

Be quhilk men ar conuertit speciallie
Frome Sin and Uice, and frome Ydolatrie,

to godliness.
Ephe. v.
Col. iii.

To godlynes, quhairin the Lord delyts,   400
As Paule in his Epistills plainlie dyts.

If we bear this fruit, it shows we are branches of the true vine, Christ.
Ioan. xv.

¶ Thir Godlie fruts dois also notefie,
Gyf we the faithfull and Germane branchis be
Of Christ Iesus, quha is the onlie wyne,   404
That did Redeme our Saul[i]s all frome pyne.

They who do not bear this fruit are grafts of Satan.
Math. v.

¶ Quho wants thir fruts, lat thame all talking stanche,
And never compt thaim of Christ to be a branche,
Bot lat thaim grant thaim branchis, Imps, & sperks
To be of Sathan, seing thair sinfull werks   409

II. 2. B. a.
A Denunciation of Hypocrites and (β.) covetous Protestants.

¶ ANE EXCLAMATIOUN AGANIS ALL FEN3EIT YPO-
CREITIS, AND SPECIALLIE AGANIS
ALL GREDIE DISSEMBLIT FALS
PROTESTANTES.

Fie on you professors who
Mathew. xxiii.
sin openly!

O Fie on 3ow that callis 3our selffs professours,
Syne notit ar for manifest transgressours !
Gods wourd is heauylie sclanderit for 3our caus, [B 1, back]
Seing 3e do nothing obserue his Lawis !   413

Ye scare the weakling from the Word.

3e skar the wayklings from the wourd receauyng,
Throw 3our vngodlie and vicius behauyng !

Ye make the poor say, 'God keep us from this profession!'

¶ Quhat sayis the pure, behalding 3our transgression?
"Grit God preserue ws from this lewd profession !   417
"Is this Gods wourd that learnis thame this euyll?

This word must come from the Devil; it can't be from God!

"It semis rather this wourd cummis of the Deuyll !
"Wer it Gods wourd, we mycht rycht weill be sure,
"Tha wald nocht in sic deuylrie indure,   421

Ye are puft up with pride!

"¶ Puft vp in pryde, sik as wes neuer sene
"Before with ony mortall mannis Eine."
Moir grit expens is maid, as I suppose,   424

Upon ane pair of prophane Monstruus hose,
Nor wald do cleith ane hundreth of the pure
That gois nakit, begging frome dure to dure.
Salyke sic Pryde pertenis to trew teaching, 428
Or ony poynt of the Appostill*is* preaching!

¶ The Godlie aucht nocht to hald vile pryde in pryce,
Seing it is the Mother of all vyce,
Quhairof proceidis all distructioun, 432
And bring[i]s Kingdomes to confusioun.

¶ For Pryde, Lucypheir fro*m* Heauinnis glore he fell,
And daylie is tor*m*entit in the Hell
With mony thousand*is* of his oppynnioun, 436
Throw verray pryde from Heauin wi*th* him fell doun.

¶ Pharao, for pryde, wes drownit in the Seye,
With all his Horsis and crewell Companye.

¶ Sennacherib, for all his bost and schore, 440
Wes put to flycht; syne, be his Sone forlore.

¶ And Nabuchodonezer, for his Pryde—
As Daniell dois distinclie weill discyde—
Wes, for his hicht, transformit in ane beist, [sign. C] 444
Quhill he agane of lawlynes did taist,
Granting him self to be ane mortall wicht,
And God allone to be the Lord of micht.

¶ In to the buke of Hester is declaird, 448
How on that gallous, proude Aman had prepaird
To put gude Merdocheus to the dead,
Him self wes hangit, withouttin moir remead.
This to be schort: quho list to pryde pretend, 452
May be assurde of ane mischeuous end;
And in the contrair, quha wald exaltit be,
Go learne at Christ, to lead Humelytie.

¶ 3e clois 3our ears, a*nd* turn*is* away 3our eyis, 456
Quhair 3e 3our pure and nedye brethren seyis!
3our Cheritie, it is be-cum sa cauld,
3e thole thame de but reuth, I der be bauld;
And euerie fatt Souch fed*is* a*nd* flammis ane vther!

Ye spend more on a pair of monstrous breeches than'd clothe 100 naked poor!
i Cor. xvi.

The Godly should not esteem Pride.
Eccl. x.
Tob. iiii.
Eccl. x.

Through pride, Lucifer fell to hell,
Esa. xiiii.

Exo. xiiii.
Pharaoh was drowned,

[i]i. Reg. xix
Sennacherib was put to flight,

Nebuchadnezzar was turned into a beast,—
Dani. iiii.
till he lowlied himself, and confessed that God alone was Lord;—

Haman was hanged on the gallows he'd prepared for Mordecai.
Hester [vii.]

The proud must come to a bad end.
Pro. xv[i.]
Math. [xi. 29]
Ioan. [xiii.]
Learn from Christ humility!

II. 2. B. β.
'Ye covetous! ye turn your eyes from your needy brethren! Ye let them die, while ye fat swine feed one another' (p. 26)

	Grit God thairfor will plaig that faithles futher! 461
	¶ And ȝit ȝe ar nothing of this eschamit;
Ye are not Protestants! i. Ioa. [iii] et .iiii.	Bot ȝe will all, Protestant*is* still be nemmit!
	So ar ȝe nocht! for Ihone sayis ȝe do lie. 464
Ye know not God, ye who leave the needy pitiless!	Ȝe knaw nocht God, nor ȝit his wourd trewlie,
	That seis ȝour nedie Brother in distres,
	Syne helps him nocht, bot layf*is* him mercyles.
Your greediness stinks the air!	¶ Ȝour gredynes! it stink*is* and fylis the air! 468
	I vg ȝour Murthour and Hirschip to declair!
Ye slay the poor: tho' not with knives,	For thocht ȝe sla nocht pure men with ȝour knyues,
	Ȝit with ȝour dearth ȝe tak from thame the lyues!
	¶ Quhat differs dearth frome creuell briganrye, 472
yet with hunger.	Quhen that ȝe mak the Pure for hunger dye?
It's murder without drawing blood!	No thing at all! most trewlie to conclude,
	Except of thame ȝe do nocht draw the blude;
[C [i] back]	For ȝe contryne thame,—as wyse me*n* merk*is* and seis,—
	Till one of thir two grit Extremiteis: 477
You buy up their food, and let the moneyless starve.	Till vtter hirschip, with bying of thair fude;
	And want tha money? than, schortlie to conclude,
	Thair is no credeit, bot of Necessitie, 480
	The Pure Broder, for Hunger he man die.
God sent you victuals, not to famish the poor, [M]athew. [xx]v. but to help them in their need.	¶ God send ȝow nocht *th*e Uictall of the ground
	That ȝe the pepill suld Fameis and confound;
	Bot that ȝe sould thairof gude Stewartis be, 484
	Helpand the Pure in thair necessite.
Woe be to the hoarder-up of [P]ro. xi. corn! God bless him that lets it out to the poor!	¶ Wo be till him that hurdis vp his Corne,
	Syne kepis it vp to dearth, fra morne to morne!
	Bot Gods blissing sall lycht vpon his head, 488
	That lat*is* it furth, that pure men may get bread.
Ye closers of your garners,	¶ Bot as ȝe cloise ȝour Girnall*is* frome *th*e puris,
	Quhilk*is* now thairby grit miserie induris,
God shall close the Gate of Heaven against you! [E]xod. xxii. [A]bac. ii.	So God sall cloise on ȝow, for ȝour grit Sin, 492
	His Heauinlie Porte, quhe*n* ȝe wald faine cum in.
	¶ So on this wyse quhen *tha*t ȝe scurge the pure,
God shall plague you again for it!	God sall ȝow Plaig agane for that, be sure!
	Experience daylie teachis ws of this: 495

Merk quhen ȝe please, ȝe sall nocht find it mis.
¶ I neid nocht rekkin ȝour filthye Harlotrie : *Your filthy harlotry is so public,*
  It is so knawin our alquhair, oppinlie ;
Quhilk to rehearse, It mak[i]s me abhor ! 500 *I loathe to speak of it.*
Bot as the Townis of Sodome and Gomor, *But, like Sodom and Gomorrah,*
The Creaturis and all that in thame was,
With fyre frome Heauin consumit was with as *Gene. xix.*
For that foule stinkand Sin of Lychorie, 504
Richt so, ȝe Harlotis, but dout sall Plagit be *ye shall be burnt-up with fire*
Be the grit Michtie God Omnipotent,
Except that ȝe moir spedylie repent ! *unless ye repent.*

¶ For mony ane tyme, and daylie it is sene, [C ii] *Harlots are often punished with poverty, shame, and sudden death. (p. 39)*
How sic vile harlotis for Hurdome Plagit bene
With most extreme and vrgent pouertie,
Quhilk sumtyme had of ryches grit plentie ; *Luc. xv*
Sumtyme with maist detestebill odious schame, 512 *Pro. ix[.] xxix.*
Loyssing for euer thair honour and thair fame, *Tob. ii*
And sumtyme plagit be God with suddand dead ; *i Cor. v[i.]*
But quho that list with wisedome to take head, *Pro. ix. Eccl. ix*
May daylie merk, and als perfytlie se, 516
The Harlotis oftymes plagit with all thre.

¶ Ȝit nocht wil mak thame from thair sin refrane, *Gal. v.*
  Quhill Saule & bodie be damnit to hellis pane. *Apoc. x[iv.] i Cor. [iii.]*
For tha perceaue nocht that thair Miserie, 520 *Heb. xi[i.]*
Dois licht on thame for thair Iniquytie. *Yet they will not give up their sin.*

  Bot rycht as Pharao on Godis plaigs wald not pance,
Bot thocht tha come be fortune & be chance, *They think God's plague is mere chance,*
No moir the Harlot can think his hart within, 524
That God dois plaig him for his filthie Sin,
And so as Palȝeartis in Peltrie perseueiris, *and so sin on while their strength lasts.*
Quhill of thair strenth consumit be the ȝeris.

  The pure Plewmen & laubouraris of ȝour lands, 528 *Ye grasping landlords, ye turn out your poor plowmen and labourers, to get more rent,*
  Quhen tha haue nocht to fill ȝour gredie hands,
Quhair ȝe can spye ane man to geue ȝow mair,
Ȝe schute thame furth ; syne puts ane vthir thair.
Howbeit the first haue Barnis aucht or nyne, 532 *though they have 8 or 9 children.*

	ȝe tak no thocht, thocht man and all sulde tyne ;
Then ye soon turn out your fresh tenants too:	Within few ȝeris ȝe herye him also,
to beggary !	Syne puts him furth ; to beggin most he go ;
This calls for vengeance from Heaven !	Thus schift ȝe our, in to most gredie wyse, 536
Esay. xx[ii et] iii.	The quhilk ane Uengeance frome *the* Heauin cryis.
	¶ ȝit for all this ȝe neuer ar content !
Ye have far more than your fathers. [Ecc]l. v.	Howbeit ȝe haue, be fer, moir land and rent
	Nor euer had ȝour Fatheris ȝow before ; [C ii, back] 540
[Esay v.v]iii.[1] And yet ye gape for more still !	Bot euer gredie, and gaping still for more.
And all to show-off your pride !	¶ And all this is, for to setfurth ȝour pryde !
Your households are cut down.	ȝour housis halding is down, & laid on syde :
Instead of 100 servants, you have a man and a boy !	Quhair hunders wount ȝour faders to conuoye, 544
	Now will ȝe ryde with ane man and ane boye.
Of your filthy vice, Avarice is the cause.	¶ Nocht hes the wyte of this ȝour filthie Uice
	Bot that fals gredie Idole Auerice,
	Quhilk chokkit hes ȝour harts so haillelie, 548
Ye eare not for God, or honour either !	That nothair to God nor honour ȝe haue Ee.
And yet, though ye should be rich, [Ecc]l. v. [Ps. x]ci.	¶ Grit meruell is, of ȝow that gett*is* this muk,
	Bot ȝe sould haue aboundance with gude luk.
	And ȝit we se thair dois nothing succeid, 552
ye are more empty of goods and gear than your fathers were !	Bot barrane ground, with mony frutles weid,
	Moir emptye now of warldlis gear and gude
	Nor wes ȝour Faders, that fand rycht mony fude,
	Quhilks had nocht half sa mekill for to spend, 556
	ȝit had grit ryches, and honour to thair end.
Needy, thriftless, and thread-bare are ye !	And ȝe ar nedye, thriftles, and threid-bair !
	Of wrangus gude, no better man can fair.
Why ? Because ye get goods wrongfully !	¶ Iudge ȝe ȝour selfis, in ȝour awin conscience, 560
	Quhat is the cause of ȝour grit Indigence !
[Ec]cl. viii. [Es]ay. v.	I saye for me, God will nocht send incresse
	To thame that wrangus Conqueis dois possesse !
Ye know God's word, and do the contrary.	Syne knawis Gods wourd, syne dois *the* contrarie ! 564
	How can sic pepill, with grit God fauourd be ?

[1] Woe unto them that join house to house, *That* lay field to field, Till *there be* no place, That they may be placed alone in the midst of *the* earth !

¶ We reid how Acham, be Gods commandiment,   *Joshua tells how Achan*
And be his rycht and most Iust Iudgement,   *[Io]sue. vii*
Wes stond to death, as Iosue concluds,   568   *was stoned, because he 'took*
Because he tuke of Excommunicat guds.   *of the accursed thing.'*
Gyf ȝe haue done with siclyke gudis mell,   *Have ye not done this?*
I can nocht say ; Iudge that amangs ȝour sell.   *Judge yourselves!*

¶ Quho list the Storie of Achab to persew,   [C 2] 572   *Ye know how Ahab and*
And Iesabell his wyfe, that Naboth slew   *i Reg. xx[i]*
For his wyne ȝaird, throw gredie Couatyce,   *Jezabel, for seizing Naboth's*
Thair sall ȝe find how God did plaig that Uyce,   *yard, were plagued by God;*
And maid thame both most miserablie to de   576
For thair foule Murthour and Cupeditie.

¶ Saule lost his Kingdome throw his gredines ·   *i Reg. xiii*
And riche Naball, for his grit churlyschenes   *how Saul lost his kingdom for his greediness;*
Schewin to Dauid, almaist had bene distroyit,   580   *i Reg. xv*
Gyf Abygall had nocht it weill conuoyit,   *how Nabal was nearly slain for*
And measit Dauid verray Prudentlie ;   *his churlishness, had not Abigail*
ȝit God maid Naball schortlie for to de,   *saved him; and*
And him bereft frome all his wardlie wrak,   584   *yet he died soon.*
For ony fence the churlysche Carll could mak.
As sall all wrachit Churlis layf thair geir,   *Eccl. v. et xiiii.*
And vtheris thairof sall mak mirrye cheir,   *And so all churls*
That nocht pertenit to thame be kin nor blude !   588   *shall die, and leave their*
All wrachis wrak thus endis, to conclude.   *goods to strangers to waste!*
ȝit mony of Naball*is* blude dois rest behind,   *We've many Nabals still; but*
Bot verray few of Abygall*is* to find !   *very few Abigails!*

¶ Paule dois pronunce in wourd*is* plane & euin,   592   *i Cor. v*
That Couatus men sall nocht inherit Heuin,   *et vi.*
And dois forbid that we expreslie
Suld bear the Couatus ony companie.

☞ Lo we se heir,—quhat nedis processe mair ?—   *Thus God's word shows that*
That God*is* trew wourd maist plainlie dois declair   597   *covetous men shall come to a*
That Couatus men, quhat way that euer tha wend,   *sorry end.*
Sall nocht at lenth eschaip ane sorye end.

¶ The Mes, that Idoll,—praysit be God !—is past ;   *The Mass is gone, thank God!*
Bot Couatyce, the quhilk is cum in last,   601   *Exo. xxiii.*

But the worse idol, Covetousness, has come in, and will mar everything. [A]bac. ii.	Is the worst Idoll of the twa, be fer;
	Gyf that this Idoll Rax, it will all mer,
	All will be brocht vnto confusioun, [C 2, back] 604
	Gods wourd and Lawis vnto abusioun,
	The Ciueill Iustice, sall peruertit be,
[E]xo. xxii.	Uproris sall ryse, and start vp haistelie,
No man will be at rest unless this Covetousness is banished.	No man sall leue at rest and peace with vther, 608
	Except this Idoll be banist with the tother;
	And wer we quyte of thir fals Idols baith,
	The Godlie than micht soundlie sleip but skaith.
Stop, and repent in time, or [I]oan. iii. [Mat. x.] et xv. you'll be plagued.	¶ Refrane in tyme! with speid repent and mend!
	Or God ane sudand plaig sall on ȝow send, 613
	And punysche ȝow be fer moir creuellie
	Nor Ignorant*is* befoir wes wint to be!
Unless ye mend, God will take his Holy Word from you.	¶ Without ȝe mend, maist certainlie I say ȝow, 616
	Gods holy wourd but dout sall be tane fra ȝow.
	Because with ȝow it is nothing regardit,
	Thairfor with God ȝe sall be so rewardit,
Strangers shall [I]ere .v. take away your Church,—the greatest plague that God can send.— [A]po. ix.	That vncouth Strangears of ane forene Natioun 620
	Sall disapoynt ȝour Kirk and Congregatioun,
	Quhilk is the gritest Plaig that God can send:
	This sall nocht mis! without ȝe schortlie mend,
	Ȝe sall be Plagit so, and on sik wyse, 624
Ye shall wish for death, and shall not be able to die.	That ȝe sall wysse ȝour death ane hundreth syse.
	And quhen ȝe wald, ȝit sall ȝe no wayis de;
	That death ȝe ȝairne, it sall fast frome ȝow fle.
Iere. ix. xvii. and xxviii. Hunger, pest, sword, and fire, Esa. xxiiii shall fall on you. God's word was never so truly preached; and yet never were so many ungodly men seen!	For Disobedience vnto Gods woord, 628
	Ȝe sall be Plagit with Hunger, Pest, and swourd,
	With Hirschip, Fyre, with Dearth, and Pestelence,
	Because ȝe Sin aganis ȝour Conscience;
	For God[i]s woord wes neuer moir trewlie teachit 632
	Nor it is now in mony placis preachit,
	And neuer sa mony vngodlie pepill sene
	In to this earth, sen it Inhabit bene!
	¶ Quhairfor, gyf ȝe grit God wald glorefie, [C 1] 636
Ioan. xv[ii.]	Imbrace his woord and learne to fructefie,

And lat ʒour werks and wourds aggre togidder, *Let your works agree with your words!*
That euerye man may graip, and als consider,
It is Gods woud and pure Religioun   640
That ʒe obserue in ʒour professioun.

¶ Quhat helpis it, thocht we the wourd professe, *What's the good of professing, unless you do?*
Except the Frute proceid thairof expresse? *Iac. i.*
Thus lat ʒour deids so schyne in tymes to cum,   644 *Let your deeds shine forth so that the beholders may glorify God!*
Tha sall be sene, and kend till all and sum,
That the Behaldars may crye with Ioyfull steuin,
"Grace, glore, and honour, be to the Father of Heuin!"
So quhen ʒour werks dois with ʒour wourds aggre, 648 *Ioan. xv. Works (with words) glorify God.*
No dout ʒe sall the Father glorefie.

¶ The secund proffit, rycht as our Text it merks, *I've thus set forth the 2nd profit from godly works,*
Tuytching the bringing furth of Godlie werks,
With faithfull Pepill that dois thair God regaird, 652
Semplie I haue heir in few wourds declaird,
So that thair rests of this mateir no mair,
Bot the thrid proffit onlie to declair, *and pass on to the 3rd.*
Quhilk schortlie now, be Gods grace, I sall end: 656
Gyf ear*is* heirfor, and to my wourds attend! *Attend to me!*

¶ FOLLOWIS THE THRID PROFFIT OF THAME   *II. 2. C.*
THAT ABYDIS IN TO CHRIST.

¶ THE TEXT.

¶ AND BE MAID MY DISCYPLIS.

THe thrid and Finall last Commoditie, *The 3rd profit is: we shall be true Ioan. xv disciples of Christ.*
'The trew Discyplis of Christ we sall all be
That bydis in Christ, & Christs wourd in to thame:'
My Text, this Sentence plainlie dois declame,   661

¶ Be the quhilk wourd*is*, merking the circumstance, *We must continue in Him to the end. Ioan. xv.*
Heir is requyrit ane ferme contynewance
In to Gods woud, compleitlie to our end,   664
Gyf we his trew Discyplis wald be kend.

¶ Inconstant men, my Text heir plane declaris, [C 1, b'k] *Inconstant men are not Christ's true scholars;*
Nane for to be, of Christ*is* trew Scolaris;

but those who'll confirm His doctrine with their blood,	Bot tha ar Christ Discyplis, to conclude,	668
	That will conferme his Doctrine wi*th* thair blude,	
	As quhen it cu*m*mis to that Extremite,	
	For to Renunce Christ*is* Uangell, or to de,	
	And chusis than to suffer fyre and swourd	672
rather than renounce His heavenly word.	Rather nor to renunce his Heauinly wourd,	
	¶ As did the Prophet*is*, and Mertyris mony one	
	With the Appostill*is*, in to the dayis bygone ;	
We have seen right many die for Christ,	And in our dayis rycht mony we did se	676
	For Christ*is* wourd do suffer pacientlie	
who might have had life, money, wives and bairns	Maist cruell death, and mycht haue had thair lyues,	
	With ȝeirlie rent*is* to thame, thair barnis & wyues,	
to give Him up.	Gyf tha the wourd of God wald haue refusit :	680
But they chose bitter death.	Tha did nocht swa, bot bitter death tha chusit.	
And they shall [ii] Cor. i. have part with Christ in Heaven,	¶ All thir Discyplis hes this rewaird heirfore,	
	Tha sall haue pairt with Christ in Heauinnis glore,	
	As dois the promeis of Christ till ws propone	684
	In the Euangell of the Apostill Ihone,	
[I]oan. xvii	Quhair, to the father, Christ speykand speciallie,	
	Saya*n*d thir wourds, " quhom thow hes geuin to me,	
as He wills ;	" I will that tha thair be with me also,	688
and shall see His glory,	" And se my glore in Heauin, quhair I sall go."	
	So this last proffit the rest dois fer transcend,	
without end.	That is Eternall, and neuer sall haue end.	
	¶ Suld lose of gud[i]s, lyfe, or feir of pyne,	692
Math. x.	Mak ws this Heauinlie Thesaure for to tyne ?	
	Quhat is it wourth to man, to win but more,	
Mat. xvi.	The haill warld, wanting the Heauinnis glore ?	
All earthly things pass away. Heaven abides, and is only to be won by those in whom God's word takes rest.	¶ All earthlie things, tha ar bot transitorie,	696
	Except this Heauinlie and Celestiall glorie,	
	Quhilk be no vther meanis can be possest,	[sign. D]
	Except Gods wourd in to our hart*is* tak rest.	
Death comforts the good,	¶ That death to man, it is grit consolatioun,	700
	The quhilk dois lead the Saule vnto saluatioun ;	
but terrifies the damned.	Bot verray feirfull and dolent is that dead	
	That dois the Saule vnto Damnatioun lead.	

¶ With Deligence now lat ws all heirfore 704 Diligently then let us embrace Christ,
Imbrace Christ Iesus, that we may cum to glore,
And in tymes cumming lat none so ernistlie pance
On earthlie glore, that lestis bot ane glance;
Bot lat our laubour, studie, and Meditatioun, 708 and let all our study be to seek our salvation, and know that none can serve God and Mammon too.
Be euer bent to seik for our Saluatioun;
And deiplie in our hartis lat ws considder,
None can serue God & Mammone boith togidder.

☞ Wo worth the landis, the gudis, gear, and flesche, Woe to the goods and flesh that draw us from Christ!
That dois man frome this heuinlie glore depesche! 713
To the quhilk glore, now breiflie to conclude,
Mot bring ws Christ, that bocht ws with his blude!

   So be it.   716

¶ Glore, Honour, Prayse, and Laude, Eternallie,
To God, for this Pure Werk! and none to me,
   ¶ Quod Lauder.

The Lamentatioun

OF THE PURE. TWICHING THE MISERABILL ESTAIT OF
THIS PRESENT WARLD. COMPYLIT BE WILLIAM
LAUDER. AT PERTH. PRIMO FABRUARIE.

1568.

[How lange, Lorde, sall this warld indure?]

<small>The world is full of mischief.</small>

THis warld is war nor euer it was!
    Full of myscheif, and all malure;
    Fals and fragell as the glas!
    How lang, Lorde, sall this warld indure?   4

<small>Professors will not help God's word.</small>

¶ For mony dois God*is* worde profes,   [sign. D, back]
    Bot for to keip it, few takis cure,
Thay ar so bent to weikitnes!
    How lang, Lord, wyll this warld indure?   8

<small>Fat sows feed one another and don't pity the poor.</small>

¶ Now euerie fat Sow feidis ane vther[1],
    And few hes pitie on the Pure;
Couatice gydis and rewlis the Ruder:
    How lang, Lord, wyll this warld indure?   12

<small>The rich abhor the poor: Protestants too!</small>

¶ The men quhome God hes rychelie dotit,
    Abhorris the emptye Creature,
Cheiflie Protestantes, lat ws notit[2]
    How lang, Lord, wyll, this warld indure?   16

---

[1] See above, p. 17, l. 460.   [2] note it.

¶ Ʒit ar nocht thir Protestantes trew,
   Bot Ipocretis, I am most sure,
That hes renuncit Christ Iesu :
   How lang, Lord, wyll this warld indure ?   20

Hypocrites they are, who have renounced Christ.

¶ Frome fraude, [frome[1]] falset, and frome gyle,
   No Preaching can the pepill allure :
Lawtie and luife ar in exile :
   How lang, Lord, wyll this warld indure ?   24

Loyalty and love are banished.

¶ Hipocrasie, vaine Glore, and Pryde,
   Now blawis thair Bugillis strang and sture ;
Simplysitie is sett on syde :
   How lang, Lord, wyll this warld indure ?   28

Vain Glory and Pride blow their bugles.

¶ The reuth that Papistis hes, I saye,
   On thame that beggis frome dure to dure,
Sall ws accuse on Domesdaye :
   How lang, Lord, wyll this warld indure   32

The Papists' charity shall accuse us at Doomsday!

¶ Now mony vsis Sosserie,
   Doand the deuylis of Hell coniure,
Seikand to knaw how all sulde be :   [D 1; no sig.]
   How lang, Lord, wyll this warld indure ?   36

People practise sorcery, conjuring up the devils of Hell.

¶ Iustice is rowpit, as vtheris waris ;
   This is most plane, and nocht obscure,
The puré Pepill it declaris :
   How lang, Lord, wyll this warld indure ?   40

Justice is sold to the highest bidder.

¶ The falsest Actioun that may be,
   Sall no wayis want ane Procuture ;
The Deuyll, he wyll get one for fe :
   How lang, Lord, wyll this warlde indure ?   44

The Devil finds an attorney to push the falsest action.

¶ Loude leand Lowreis, for thair sleuth
   Was treatit, passing throw mosse and Mure :
Upon trew Preacheour*is* few hes reuth :
   How lang, Lord, wyll this warld indure ?   48

Loud-lying Foxes are cared for; true Preachers passed over.

[1] *or read* fraud-e.

Trust is gone.
 Usury rules:
 2d. for 1d.!
	¶ Credit and frist is quyte away,
	     No thing is lent bot for Usure;
	 For euerie penny thay wyll haue tway:
	     How lang, Lord, wyll this warld indure?
		52

Old good deeds are forgotten.	¶ For auld kyndnes thow sall nocht get
	     Bot Magerie, Malice, and Iniure;
	 Auld gude done dedis ar quyte forʒet:
	     How lang, Lord, wyll this warld indure?
		56

Dainty Dames won't support the faithful.	¶ The dayntie Dammis may nocht sustene
	     The faithfull, for to fyle thair flure,
	 Bot treatis thame *that* tryit trumpour*is* bene:
	     How lang, Lord, wyll this warld indure?
		60

Flatterers, Bards, Brothel-haunters, are treated best.	¶ Ane fenʒeit flatterair or Fuile, I say,
	     Ane Barde, ane Bragger, or Bordell Hure;
	 Ar none treatit so weill as thay:
	     How lang, Lord, wyll this warld indure?
		64

Nothing on earth is worse than pride in a Minister.	¶ In all the earth is no thing wer [D 1, back]
	     In to no earthlie Creature,
	 Nor heicht into ane Minister:
	     How lang, Lord, wyll this warld indure?
		68

Papists are more liberal to one another than some Ministers are.	¶ ʒit Papistis bearis ilke ane to vther
	     More liberall luife, I am moste sure,
	 Nor dois sum Minister to his Brother:
	     How lang, Lord, wyll this warld indure?
		72

Daughter and son scorn father and mother.	¶ And now the Dochter and the Sone
	     Lichtlyis the Mother that thame bure,
	 And forʒettis quhat thair Father hes done:
	     How lang, Lord, wyll this warld indure?
		76

For all this ill, God's word is not to blame.	¶ Of this Iniure and dispyte
	     Wrocht of all cankerit Creature,
	 I saye God*is* wourd hes nocht the wyte:
	     How lang, Lord, wyll this warld indure?
		80

¶ For to behauld this Miserie,   *My heart burns to see all this misery.*
  My breist in baill it dois combure,
Sen reuth is none, nor ȝit Pitie:
  How lang, Lord, wyll this warld indure?   84

¶ Sen all Estaitis this[1] gois astray,   *Surely, God will plague us for it soon.*
  Lat no man think bot this is sure,
That God wyll Plaig ws but delay,
  For thus we can nocht lang indure.   88

¶ Quhairfore, lat euerie Creature,   *Let us all, then, pray that we may all embrace the Light of Heaven!*
  The Mercyis of grit God procure,
That we may ones[2] Inbrace the Lycht
  Of Heauin, quhilk euer sall indure.   92

¶ FINIS.

Quod Lauder.

[1] thus: see p. 9, l. 205.   [2] at once.

Ane prettie Mirrour

Or Conference, betuix the faithfull Protestant and the Dissemblit false Hypocreit. In to the quhilk may be maist easylie perceaued & knawin the one from the vther. Compylit be William Lauder Minister of the word of God. For the Instructioun, Comfort, and Consolatioun of all Faithfull Professours. To quhome he wyssith Grace Mercy and Peace, in Jesus Christ our Lord, and onlie Saviour. So be it.

Luke in to this Mirrour, and thow sall cleirlie ken
All faithfull trew Christianes, from fals dissemblit men.

To the faithful Reder.

[leaf 1, back.]

These verses are sweet to the Godly, but odious to the Vicious.

Hir Uearse ar sweit and rycht delicius
   Unto the hart*is* of Godlie men, I ken;
But to the weked tha ar rycht odius,
And comptit folie w*ith* all vnfaithful men.   4

They show the ways of the Godly, and the vice of the Wicked.

¶ For of the Godlie, tha schew the trade and ways,
   How tha thame self*is* heir vpon earth dois gyde;
And of the weked, thair vice and grit decaye;
   Quhilk manassing tha can no wayis abyde.   8

Let each man examine himself, and if he is guilty, repent.

¶ Humblie heirfore I walde ilk man exhort
   Thame self to trye[1] out, be this subsequent,
Gyf vice or virtew dois maist in thame resort: 11
   Quha find*is* him gyltie, God gra*n*t he may repent!
              So be it.

[1] crye *in orig.*

Begynnis the Conferrence.

The chosin children of God, and sones elect,
 Reiosis cheiflie to heir his blissit wourd :
The sons of satha*n*, quhilk*is* ar fro*m* God reiect,
 Abhorris *tha*t same more nor ane two edgits wourd.

The Chosen rejoice in God's word, Satan's sons abhor it.

¶ The Godlie will with pacience Imbrace   17
 Dew Admonitioun for thair vice and sin :
The wekit can nocht, in the contrair cace,
 Sustene reproche, syne byde thair witt*is* within.

The Godly take rebuke patiently, the Wicked do not.

¶ The godlie will in to gude pairt sustene,   21
 Dew chaistisment for thair Sin and offence :
Punysche the wekit, tha will alwayis complene,
 As geue tha wer opprest be violence.   24

The Godly take chastisement humbly, [leaf 2] the Wicked complain.

¶ The godlie men with pietie ar opprest
 To see thair Brethren in necessitie :
The Hypocreit*is* ar neuer at ease nor rest
 But quhen the faithfull sustenis miserie.   28

The Godly pity the poor : the Hypocrites exult in the misery of the Faithful.

¶ The Godlie men will do no man bakbyte,
 Nowthair in patent nor in to priuie place :
In blasphemie the wekit dois delyte,
 And frome Iniurie his toung can neuer cease.   32

The Godly do not backbite ; the Wicked delight in blasphemy.

¶ The Godlie man will vse no mokkerie,
 And will no wayis with sic vaine maters mell :
The Hypocreit will skorne contynewallie,
 And neuer can finde ane falt in to him sell.   36

The Godly do not mock ; the Hypocrites always scorn others.

¶ The Godlie men will vse no fraude nor gylis,
 And will be laith to sute men to the law :
The Hypocreit*is* ar euer breding wylis,
 And passing how, thair broder to owrthraw.   40

The Godly use no frauds, the Hypocrites ever breed wiles.

¶ The Godlie men ar full of gentilnes,
 Of Lawtie, Loue, and liberalitie :
The Hypocreit*is* ar full of gredines,
 Of Aueryce, and Pegeralitie.[1]   44

The Godly are full of love ; the Hypocrites of avarice.

---

[1] Lat. *piger*, reluctant, unwilling, averse. *Pegrall :* Lyndesay.

The Godly feed the poor;	¶ The Godlie men, tha do support the pure,
	And geuis thame glaidlie of thair geir a*n*d gude :
the Hypocrites rob them.	The Hypocreit*is* dois take more thocht and cure
	How tha may reaue fro*m* thame thair daylie fude.
The Godly are content in woe and weel;	¶ The Godlie men Elykewise ar content, 49
	Als weill in neid as in prosperitie :
[leaf 2, back] the Hypocrites in need curse God.	The Hypoccreit*is*, quhe*n* geir is frome thame went,
	Tha blaspheme God in thair aduersitie. 52
The Godly hate sin,	¶ The Godlie men detest*is* all vice and Sin,
	And all transgressour*is* and thair companie :
the Hypocrites delight in it.	The Hypocreit*is*, tha do delyte thairin,
	Leading thair lyues in all Impietie. 56
The Godly take no bribes;	¶ The Godlie men, no brybs nor buds¹ will take,
	To hurt the ane pairt, nor to helpe the vther :
the Hypocrites do.	The Hypocreit will thinke no schame nor lak,
	Buds to receaue, and tha wer fra his broder. 60
The Godly serve one God;	¶ The Godlie men will serue ane God allone,
	Quhilk maker is of Heauin, the earth, and seye :
the Hypocrites many.	The Hypocret*is* mak*is* gods mony one,
	With quhome tha do commit Idolatrie. 64
The Godly are true in their dealings;	¶ The Godlie men in all thair wayis ar plaine,
	And cheiflie euer onto thair faithfull brother :
the Hypocrites are false.	The Hypocreit*is* ar fenʒeit, fals, and vaine ;
	Will saye ane thing, and syne will do ane vther.
The Godly are lowly and lovi.ng;	¶ The Godlie ar repleit with lawlynes, 69
	With louyng kyndnes, and humelytie :
the Hypocrites proud and spiteful.	The Hypocreit*is*, thocht tha it nocht expres,
	Ar full of hic*h*t, dispyte, and tyrannie. 72
The Godly labour for peace;	¶ The Godlie labours for vnitie and peace,
	For concorde, kyndnes, and tranquilytie :
the Hypocrites for strife.	The Hypocreit*is* dois neuer stanche nor cease
	To rais discorde and Innanymitie. 76

¹ *Bud*, a gift; generally one that is meant as a bribe. *Acts, Ja. I.*, in Jamieson.

ANE PRETTIE MIRROUR.

The Godlie luffis thair Pastours, for thair cure,   *The Godly love their Pastors;*
   And will be sorie to se thame want or wrangt :
The Hypocreit*is* regairds nocht, we ar sure,   *[leaf 3] the Hypocrites would like to see 'em hanged.*
   Thocht all the preachours on *th*e earth wer hangt.
The Godlie men will still cleue to Gods wourd,   81   *The Godly are true to the death;*
   Thocht tha to death for it suld be persewit :
The Hypocreit, sa sone as cu*m*mis the swourd,   *the Hypocrites soon deny the Faith.*
   Will it denye, and sweir he neuer knewit.[1]   84

The Godlie men setts God before all things,   *The Godly set God first;*
   Before thair lyues, thair guds, [&] geir, or lands :
The Hypocreit*is*, before God puts thair kings,   *the Hypocrites despise Him.*
   Dispysing God, his lawis, and his commands.   88

The Godlie men ar knawin be thir merks,   *The Godly are known by these marks;*
   Rycht as the daye is tryit be the lycht :
Euin so the wekit, be thair vicius werks   *the Wicked by their dark deeds.*
   Ar so espyit, as derknes schewis the nycht.   92

For as no wayis, the fyre, it can be knawin   *No fire can be without heat;*
   To be ane fyre, withouttin heit or lycht :
No more *th*e faithfull, except gude werks be schawin,   *not Godly without good works.*
   Can notit be for to be Christianes rycht.   96

The preist, & Leueit, *th*e quhilk did nocht support   *Luc. x. The Priest and Levite were not faithful;*
   The woundit man in to his greif and paine,
Could nocht be comptit faithful in no sort   *Luc. xvi.*
   As was the helpfull trew Samaritaine.   100   *like the good Samaritan.*

Nor ȝit the Gluttoun, quha fed delicius,   *Nor was the glutton Dives,*
   Could nocht be said to haue fidelytie,
That petiit nocht the puré Lazarus,   *who pitied not Lazarus so much*
   Quhen Dogs did schew in him more cherytie.   104   *as the dogs did,*

Q[u]hairthrow *th*e Gluttoun vnto the hell was sent,   *and was first sent to Hell,*
   That had no reuth nor pietie on the pure :
All Hypocreitts that lykewise dois offend,   *[leaf 3, back] where all Hypocrites shall go too.*
   With him in Hell sall harbreit be most sure.   108

[1] knew it.

ANE PRETTIE MIRROUR.

We boast ourselves Christians; but if we do not good works, we are very Hypocrites.

¶ Thus, thocht we boist, Christianes to be,
    Except gude werks proceid out of our spreits,
We ar bot membris of Iniquytie,
And ar nocht els bot verray Hypocreits.   112

Let us show forth good works; and be known as God's servants!

¶ Lat ws heirfore schew furth with al our mycht
    Our godlie werks of mercy and of loue :
Quhairthrow we may be kend of euery wycht,   115
    The faithfull seruands of God that rings aboue.

Let us mortify all lewd affections, and force our enemies to call us Christians.

¶ Lat leud affectionis and all Impieteis
    Be mortefiit in to our membris all,
That tha may nocht, quhilks ar our Inymeis,
    No vther thing bot Christianes ws call.   120

Ye Godly, rejoice!
God has chosen you!
Wicked! Repent or be lost!

¶ Godlie, heirfore Reioyse, that hes thir sings ![1]
    ȝe may be sure that God hes ȝow elect !
Bewaill, ȝe weked, that in sick vicis rings ![2]
    But ȝe repent, the Lord hes ȝow reiect !   124

Godly! Stand firm!

¶ All ȝe, heirfore, that hes Gods wourd profest,
    And maid with God and man, that blyssit band,
Stand ferme and stable, gyf ȝe wald cum to rest,

The fan is near at hand.

    for now the Fan approchis fast at hand.[3]   128

Let nothing of this world make you shrink back!

¶ Se that no ryches, nor wardlie pomp nor glore,
    Mak ws schrink bak now frome the veritie !
And quho so dois, to thair grit schame but more,
    God will disclose thair vile Hypocresie.   132

O God! defend Thy flock!

¶ Eternall God ! thy faithfull flok defend !
    Preserue thame, Lord, for now and euer more !

Send them Thy peace!

And grace, and peace, vnto thy subiects send,
    That seiks nocht els, bot to set furth thy glore !

Quod William Lauder.

[1] these signs.   [2] in whom such vices reign.
[3] 'I indeed baptize you with water unto repentance : but he that cometh after me is mightier than I, whose shoes I am not worthy to bear : he shall baptize you with the Holy Ghost, and *with* fire : whose fan *is* in his hand, and he will thoroughly purge his floor, and gather his wheat into the Garner ; but he will burn up the chaff with unquenchable fire.' John the Baptist, in *Matthew* iii. 11, 12. See also *Luke* iii. 16, 17.

Ane trew & brewe Sen-
encius Discriptioun of yᵉ nature of Scotland Twi-
ching the Interteinment of virtewus men That laketh
Ryches. Compyld be William Lauder, Minister of
Gods wourd. &c.

[leaf 4]

Howbeit thow war of portrature preclair,
    And war indewit w*ith* prignant virteuis seir,
    And thocht i*n* knawledge *thou* had no compair,
    That thou culd teache all sciencis perqueir,   4
 And thocht of blude thow war ane prencis peir,
Ȝit in this Realme, I Lat the vnderstand,
    And thow Layk substance of thy awin, and geir,
Thow will be Lytill regardit in this Land.   8

¶ Bot thocht thow be ane Ideote, or ane fule,
    Ane maykles monstour, withoutin wit or lair,
    Ane Blunt bubo, that neuer had bene at scule,
    And sik as Is of euerye virtew bair,   12
 Ȝit haue thow gud*is* and geir, I the declair,—
Thoucht thow be weked, I put the out of dout,—
    And thocht thow war to sathane, Sone & air,
Ȝit for thy bag*is* thow sall be takin owt.   16

Though you are handsome, virtuous, peerless in knowledge,

and nobly born, yet here, if you lack gear, you'll be little regarded.

But if you're an idiot, a monster of a fool, a stupid owl, without a virtue,

wicked,

Satan's own son, yet, if you've bags, you'll be well received.

THE INTERTENIMENT OF VIRTEWUS MEN.

Alas! The virtuous poor are of no worth:

beasts, for bags, are in authority!

The cause is Covetousness.

Alas! Alas!

¶ Allace ! heir is ane Cairfull Miserie !
 That virtewis men but geir ar of no pryce,
And Beasts, for bags, ar in Authorytie !
 I think this change is wonderus strange & nyce !
 The caus heirof Is onlie Couattyse,   21
That blinds so man that he can no wayis se
 To cheryse virtew, And ay chaistyce vice :
Allace ! heir is ane cairfull misere !   24

quod Lauder.

[leaf 4, back] ¶ Neathir virtew nor wit, in to this weked land
Doith proffeit thame that hes nocht gud*is* in ha*n*d.

☞ ANE GVDE EXEMPILL. ☜

[leaf 4, back]

BE THE BUTTERFLIE, INSTRUCTING MEN

TO HAIT ALL HARLOTTRIE.[1]

The Butterflie, hir self for to distroye,
 Upone the nycht to flie Scho dois nocht stint
Unto the candle,—scho taks thairof sick Ioye,—
Quhill scho hirself in to the Flam haue brint.   4
My tender freind, this in thy hart thow hint
And haue It euer in thy momorye :
Quha hants Hurdome, no dout be sall be tint,
And Birne him self, as dois the Butterflie.   8

margin: As the butterfly flies at night into the candle till she's burnt; so, young friend, remember that the Whorer shall be lost and burnt. i. Cor. vi [xvii]

The sapient salomon, with wemen was confoundit,
 Thocht he was wysest that euer nature wrocht ;
The force of Samson, that in to strenth aboundit,
 Be Dalyla was suttellie out socht ;   12
The Propheit Dauid, full deir his loue he bocht,
With mony mo that vsit sick vaniteis,
 Was dyuers wayis vnto confusioun brocht,
And Brint thame selffs, as dois the Butterfleis.   16

margin: iii. Reg. xi. By women, Eccle. .xlvij. Sap. vii. viii. Solomon was Iud. xvi. and .xiiij. confounded, .ii. Regum. xi. Samson lost his strength, and David suffered.

---

[1] See above, p. 19.

	¶ Quhairfor, my freinds, from fantasie refraine !
Math. v.	
Exod. xx.	Detest that Sin of vice and vanytie,
My friends,	
Liuic. xix.	Quhilk saule & bodie both dois bring to paine !
keep from and	
Deu. xxv.	Fle frome that lust, as frome ȝour Inymie ! 20
Pro. xxix.	Syne, in this mateir, merk the Moralytie,
detest that sin	
i. Cor. vi.	And lat it be to ȝow ane trew Instructioun,
and .vii.	Thay may be all compard vnto this Flie,
and lust!	
Its followers	That wylfullie dois wirk thair awin Distructioun. 24
will be burnt like	
the butterfly.	
	¶ Thocht men in Mariage, with thair maiks repair
If married men	
decently use	
their wives,	In Decent maner, no man suld It reproue,
let no man	
Math. xix.	For of that Band God was the Minister,
reprove this :	
God ordained it to	Ordand of him for our wealth and behoue. 28
make men hate	
harlotry.	Sen this Command we haue frome God aboue,
i. Cor. vi.	
and .vii.	Cheiflie for this, to hait all Harlottrie,
Let, then, all	Lat euerie one chuse thame thair lauchfull Loue,
who haven't	
the gift of	That lakis that Holy gyft of Chaistetie. 32
chastity, choose	
a lawful Love.	

Quod William Lauder, Minister.

[There are some marks at the right corner of the foot of the
  page, which look at first like part of a catchword, but which
  a practised bibliographer, whom I askt about them, reads
  'ende'. I supposed them to be ink-marks.]

NOTES:

JSTIFICATIONS OF THE BIBLICAL AND OTHER REFERENCES PARED OFF Y THE BINDER OF THE GODLIE TRACTATE, AND RE-INSERTED BY THE REV. WALTER GREGOR OF PITSLIGO MANSE, ROSEHEARTY, BY FRASERBURGH, ABERDEENSHIRE.

Line 41. Math. [v.] 18. For verily I say unto you, Till heaven and earth pass, one jot or one tittle shall in no wise pass from the law, till all be fulfilled.

l. 42. 1 Peter [iv.] 11. If any man speak, let him speak as the oracles of God.

l. 43-46. Isa. lvi[ii.] 1. Cry aloud, spare not, lift up thy voice like a trumpet, and shew my people their transgression, and the house of Jacob their sin.

l. 68. [G]al. ii. and [iii.]. The whole chapter is against the doctrine of salvation by works.

l. 75. [J]aco. i. Verse 8 is applicable, "A double-minded man is unstable in all his ways."

l. 280. Mar. vi[ii.] 31. And he began to teach them, that the Son of man must suffer many things, and be rejected of the elders and of the chief priests, and scribes, and be killed, and after three days rise again.

l. 281. Ioan xv[i.] 28. I came forth from the Father, and am come into the world: again I leave the world, and go to the Father.

l. 283-4. Ioan xv[i.] 7. Nevertheless I tell you the truth: It is expedient for you that I go away: for if I go not away, the Comforter will not come unto you; but if I depart, I will send him unto you.

l. 295. Ioan vi[i.] 34. Ye shall seek me, and shall not find me.

l. 309-312. *Berengarius* and *Hugo*. [Hug]o Be[ren]g. de [Tour]se. The true doctrine of Transubstantiation was first propounded by Paschasius Radbert of Corbey, in his work " de corpore et sanguine Domini," addressed to the Emperor Charles the Bald, between the years 830 and 832. This doctrine was generally adopted as orthodox, till towards the middle of the eleventh century, when Berengar, Canon of Tours, and afterwards Archdeacon of Angers, called it in question in a letter addressed to Lanfranc, first, abbot of St Stephen in Caen, and afterwards archbishop of Canterbury. Berengar was condemned at Rome, 1050, under Leo X., without a hearing. This condemnation was repeated the same year at Vercelli. In 1054 another Council was held at Tours; but, with the help of Gregory VII., Berengar was protected from the fury of his enemies. In 1059 another Council was held at Rome, at which he was condemned through the violent conduct of Humbert, and compelled to subscribe a confession of faith drawn up by Humbert, in which he professed to believe, " panem et vinum, quæ in altari ponuntur, post consecrationem, non solum sacramentum, sed etiam verum corpus et sanguinem Domini nostri Jesu Christi esse, et sensualiter, non solum sacramento, sed in veritate, manibus sacerdotum tractari, frangi, et fidelium dentibus atteri."

Hugo St Victor, an Augustinian canon in the monastery of St Victor at Paris, was born either at Ypres or in Lower Saxony in the year 1096. He was one of the most learned men of the age, and one of the profoundest thinkers. His aim was to combine scholasticism with mysticism. He was called by his contemporaries " alter Augustinus" and " lingua Augustini." His principal work is entitled:— De sacramentis fidei Christianæ, Ll. II.

l. 311-12. [Colo]s. ii. The whole chapter is on union with Christ. Verse 19: And not holding the Head, from which all the body by joints and bands having nourishment ministered, and knit together, increaseth with the increase of God.

l. 455. Ioan [xiii.] 4-17. Christ washing the disciples' feet.

l. 511. Prov. ix[.] This may be for vi. or vii.: vi. 23, 29, or vii. 6-23. [Verse 18 of ch. ix. is meant by Lauder's l. 514; but in his first reference to Luke xv. (the Prodigal Son), the elder son's words, ' as soon as this thy son was come, which hath *devoured thy living with harlots*,' may point to the literal meaning of the '*bread eaten in secret*' of Prov. ix. 17.

13 A foolish woman *is* clamorous:
    She is simple, and knoweth nothing.
14 For she sitteth at the door of her house,
    On a seat in the high places of the city,
15 To call passengers
    Who go right on their ways:
16 Whoso *is* simple, let him turn in hither:
    And *as for* him that wanteth understanding, she saith to him,
17 Stolen waters are sweet,
    And bread *eaten* in secret[1] is pleasant.
18 But he knoweth not that the dead *are* there;
    And that her guests *are* in the depths of hell.—F. J. F.]

[1] *Heb.* of secrecies.

l. 518-19. Apoc. x[iv.] 9, 10, 11. And the third angel followed them, saying with a loud voice, If any man worship the beast and his image, and receive his mark in his forehead, or in his hand, the same shall drink of the wine of the wrath of God, which is poured out without mixture into the cup of his indignation; and he shall be tormented with fire and brimstone in the presence of the holy angels, and in the presence of the Lamb: and the smoke of their torment ascendeth up for ever and ever: and they have no rest day nor night, who worship the beast and his image, and whosoever receiveth the mark of his name.

l. 520. 1 Cor. [iii.] 3. For ye are yet carnal: for whereas *there is* among you envying, and strife, and divisions, are ye not carnal, and walk as men? See Gal. v.

l. 538-41. [Ecc]l. v. 10. He that loveth silver shall not be satisfied with silver; nor he that loveth abundance with increase.

l. 552. [Ecc]l. v. 12, 13, 14. The abundance of the rich will not suffer him to sleep. There is a sore evil *which* I have seen under the sun, *namely*, riches kept for the owners thereof to their hurt. But those riches perish by evil travail.

l. 552. [Ps. x]ci. 7-9; Ps. xcii. of the Authorized Version. When the wicked spring as the grass, and when all the workers of iniquity do flourish; *it is* that they shall be destroyed for ever: for thou, Lord, *art most* high for evermore. For, lo, thine enemies, O Lord, for, lo, thine enemies shall perish; all the workers of iniquity shall be scattered.

l. 560-64. [Ec]cl. viii. 12, 13. Though a sinner do evil an hundred times, and his *days* be prolonged, yet surely I know that it shall be well with them that fear God, which fear before him: But it shall not be well with the wicked, neither shall he prolong *his* days, *which are* as a shadow; because he feareth not before God.

l. 613. [Mat. x.] et xv. 11-15. 15. Verily I say unto you, It shall be more tolerable for the land of Sodom and Gomorrha in the day of judgment, than for that city.

l. 636. Ioan. xv[ii.] 17. Sanctify them through thy truth; thy word is truth.

ib. verse 22. And the glory which thou gavest me I have given them; that they may be one, even as we are one; I in them, and thou in me, that they may be made perfect in one.

l. 684. [2] Cor. i. 20. For all the promises of God in him are yea, and in him Amen, unto the glory of God by us.

GLOSSARY.

5/18 means page 5, line 18.

abone, 11/264, above
Abygall, 21/581, Abigail
Achab, 21/572, Ahab
Acham, 21/566, Achan
aduert, 4/32, turn to me, attend
alquhair, 19/499, everywhere
Aman, 17/449, Haman
Antechrist, 5/72
as, with, 19/503, to ashes
at, 15/369, in
at all, 9/214, at all events
Avarice, 20/547

bags, 5/75, money-bags
baill, 29/82, flame, blaze (balefire, bonfire)
baptism, 5/59
blindlynes, 13/332, blindly
bordell, 28/62, brothel
bourd, 4/40, joke
brether, 10/219, brethren
briganrye, 11/472, brigandage
brint, 3/4, burnt
bubo, 37/11, owl, stupid
buds, 34/57, 60, bids, offers, gifts, bribes, or gifts meant as a bribe
bure, 28/74, bare, bore
busse, 5/76, bush

but, 6/91, without
Butterfly and candle, p. 39-40

cairfull, 38/17, 24, full of care, of trouble
calyditie, 15/388, warmth
cassin, 6/100, cast
cearche, 11/244, search
cheryse, 38/23, cherish
combure, 29/82, burn up
compair, 37/3, compeer
conqueis, 20/563, possessions. M.Lat. *conquestus*, biens acquis, n'importe comment, par héritage, guerre, &c.—*D'Arnis*.
contryne, 18/476, scheme, drive, or constrain
couattyse, 38/21, covetousness
couatus, 21/593-8, covetous
cure, 4/46, care

Dalyla, 39/12, Delilah
daft, 12/267, foolish, mad
David, 14/350
de, 17/459, die
Dearth of 1568 A.D., p. x-xi
declame, 23/661, speak out, declare
depesche, 25/713, hinder
der, 17/459, dare

deuylrie, 16/421, devilry
disapoynt, 22/621, disestablish, take away
discyde, 3/19 (L. *discindo*, cleave asunder), discuss; 10/230, 17/443, declare
discydit, 6/83, discuss it, understand it
Dives, 7/117, 35/105
dolent, 24/702, grievous
dotit, 26/13, endowed

elec, 9/194, elect
eleckit, 9/185, elected
election, the doctrine of, p. 14-15
elykewise, 34/49, likewise
eschamit, 18/462, ashamed
esperance, 12/299, hope

falset, 27/21, falsehood
Fan, Christ's, 36/128
fence, 21/585, defence
fenʒeit, 28/61, 34/67, feigning, false
Flam, 39/4, flame
flammis, 17/460, flams, gammons, flatters. I rather imagine *flam* is a term used in cooking, to baste meat, with butter, or fat gravy, while roasting.—*D. Laing.*
force, 9/208, needs, of necessity
fordwart, 15/380, forward, further
frist, 28/49, delay, lending on trust
futher, 18/461, foother, *fudder*, a great quantity; A.S. *foðer*, mass, load; Germ. *fuder*, a wine-tun.—*Percy Folio Bal. & Rom.*, i. 172, l. 160.
fylis, 18/468, defiles

geir, 37/18, goods, money
germane, 16/403, belonging to the same germ, genuine

girnallis, 18/490, garners, granaries
glore, 6/105, glory
Glutton, the, and Lazarus, 7/117, 35/105
God-makers, Popish, 13/314
graip, 3/9, grope, feel, perceive
Greediness of the rich, 18/468
grapand, 9/188, groping, examining
gyf, 12/283, if

haill, 6/85, whole
haillelie, 20/548, wholly
hants, 39/7, practises
harbreit, 35/108, harboured, lodged
harlotry, filthy and open, 19/498, 39/30
heicht, hicht, 17/444, 28/67, 34/72, hauteur, pride
heir doun, 7/135, down here
heirfor, 3/13, for this reason
herye, 20/534, harry, rob, spoil
Hester, 17/448, (the book of) Esther
hint, 39/5, seize, take
hirschip, 18/469, 22/630, act of harrying; and its result, 18/478, need, misery
hose, 17/425, breeches (Pref. p. xxi-xxii)
hypocrites, p. 33-36

Iesabell, 21/573, Jezabel
ilkane, 11/256, each one
imps, 16/408, grafts
in, 17/454, on
indurs, 4/36, endures, continues
ingraft, 4/25, 29, engrafted
ingrauit, 10/237, engrafted
ingrauyng, 11/247, engrafting

46 GLOSSARY.

innanymitie, 34/76, enmity
in to, 4/34, in
Ihone, 18/464, St John
Iosue, 21/568, Joshua
iowking, 13/324, joking, playing tricks
Ipocretis, 27/18, hypocrites
Iusse, 6/107, juice

kend, 23/666, known as

lair, 37/10, lore, learning
landlords, greedy, 19/528, &c.
laubouraris, 19/528, labourers
lawlynes, 34/69, lowliness
lawtie, 27/23, loyalty
layfis, 18/467, leave
laykis, 12/268, despise, A.S. *wlacian*
Lazarus, 7/117
le, 12/287, lie; leis, 6/94, lies
lead, 17/455, practise
learnis, 16/418, teaches
leue in to, 8/154, believe in
leuis, 8/162, live
Levite, the, 35/97
lichtlyis, 28/74, makes light of, despises
lowreis, 27/45, lowries, foxes, crafty persons, deceivers
Lucypheir, 17/434, Lucifer
lychorie, 19/504, lechery
lyuelie, 4/39, living

Magdalene, the, 14/350
Magerie, 28/54, ? magic, conjuring; see 27/33-4
maiks, 40/25, mates, wives
malure, 26/2, *malheur*, mishap .. disaster, calamitie, miserie.—*Cotgrave*.

man, 9/208, must
man, one, and a boy, the only retinue of the rich, 20/545
maykles, 37/10, matchless
measit, 21/582, mitigated, appeased
mell, 21/570, meddle
Merdocheus, 17/450, Mordecai
mertyris, 24/674, martyrs
Messe, 5/65, Romish 'Mass,' 21/600
mischeuous, 17/453, bad, ill-finishing
mot, 25/75, may

Nabal, 21/579; modern Nabals, 21/590
Naboth, 21/573
Nabuchodonezer, 17/442
nemmit, 18/463, named, called
Nero, 7/115
nor, 11/260, than

on, 14/357, of
ones, 29/91, at once
or, 8/160, ere, before
our, 19/499, over
owrthraw, 33/40, overthrow

Paip, 11/245, Pope
Palȝeartis, 19/526, lechers. Lyndesay's *Monarche*, l. 5706. Fr. *paillard*: m. A lecher, wencher, whoremunger, whorehunter. *Paillarde*: f. A whore, punke, drab, strumpet, harlot, queane, courtezan, strumpet.—*Cotgrave*.
pance, 19/522, 25/706, pense, think
Papist, 12/285; Papisticall, 12/291
Paul, 16/401

GLOSSARY. 47

pegeralitie, 33/44, reluctance, stinginess
peltrie, 19/526, ? fornication
perqueir, 37/4, *par cœur*, by heart, accurately (*Jamieson*)
persewit, 35/82, persecuted
peruerst, 5/64, perverse
Peter, 14/350
Pharaoh, 7/116, 17/438
plat, 7/131, plainly, flat
plead, 6/91, debate, discussion
plewmen, 19/528, ploughmen
port, 7/146, 18/493, gate
precellit, 13/317, excelled
Pride, p. 17, 27/25
professors, 16/410
puris, 18/490, poor people
Pussant, for *puissant*, 4/44, powerful

quhidder, 9/212, whether
quhilk, the, 5/52, who
quhill, 12/282, til

rax, 22/603, rule (? A.S. *ricsian*)
reieckit, 7/128, reiect, 36/124, rejected
reif, 14/343, robbery
retreattabill, 4/41, withdrawable
Reuth (but), 17/459, without pity
Rin (the), 5/58, they run
ring, 12/297, reign. *Ring* is still the pronunciation of Banffshire.— *W. Gregor*
ringand, 15/393, reigning
rowpit, 27/37, sold (by auction). See Lyndesay's *Satyre* on the Judges, p. 415

Salomon, 39/9, Solomon
Salvation by works, 5/68

salyke, 17/428, so likely!
Samaritan, the Good, 35/100
Sampson, 39/11
sapour, 6/107, 110, juice, sap (*Georgics*, iv. 267)
schaifling, 13/322, shaveling, tonsured man
schore, 17/440, threatening
schrinkars, 5/74, shrinkers
schute, 19/531, shoot, thrust
seir, 37/2, several, various
sen, 3/14, since ; 13/330, that
Sennacherib, 17/440
sensyne, 12/286, since
sings, 36/121, signs
sosserie, 27/33, sorcery
souch, 17/460, sow, 26/9
sperit, 12/289, asked
sperks, 16/408, spots, portions
spye, 19/530, perceive
stanche, 34/75, stop
steuin, 23/646, voice
stint, 39/2, stop
subieckit with, 14/341, subjected to, subdued by
syse, 22/625, sithes, times

temporesars, 5/73, temporizers
tha, 5/51, they
Thesaure, 24/693, treasure
thir, 5/56 (*pron.*), these
this, 9/205, 10/219, 29/85, thus
thole, 7/136, suffer ; tholit, 8/159
til, 1/2, to
tinsall, 5/78, loss
trade, 32/5, *not* (says Mr Murray) 'treading, path, course, life,' but 'conduct (still used in this sense), trade, business, as Fr. *affaire*, to-do, doings, conduct, operations
treatis, 28/59, treat, entertain

trumpouris, 28/59, deceivers
tryis, 8/175, for 'cries'
tykis, 9/203, dogs
tyne, 20/533, be lost, perish

uaill, 8/172, vale
Vangell, 24/671, evangel, gospel
Uicar, 14/352, Vicar
vomatiue, 9/203, vomit
vptake, 8/155, take up
Usure, 28/50, usury

war, 26/1, worse
wardlie, 8/158, worldly
waykling, 16/414, weakling
Weked, wekit, 9/183, &c.; 32/3, 7, &c, wicked

wicht, 17/446, wight, creature
widderit, 6/98, withered
will God, 3/20, if God will, God willing, *Deo volente*
wine, 16/395, vine
wint, 22/615, wont
works and words to agree, 23/638
worth, 25/712, be to
wraith, 8/176, wrath
wrak, 8/176, take vengeance on
wrangus, 20/559, wrongful, wrongly-gotten
wys, 11/261, wish
wyte, 20/546, blame

ʒairne, 22/627, yearn for, desire

The manufacturer's authorised representative in the EU for product safety is Oxford University Press España S.A. of el Parque Empresarial San Fernando de Henares, Avenida de Castilla, 2 – 28830 Madrid (www.oup.es/en or product.safety@oup.com). OUP España S.A. also acts as importer into Spain of products made by the manufacturer.

www.ingramcontent.com/pod-product-compliance
Lightning Source LLC
LaVergne TN
LVHW022002060526
838200LV00003B/68